AS IF SMILING
By Sharon Anderson

after speaking like this to Lord Krishna, the mighty Arjuna said to Krishna: "I shall not fight," and became silent.
Lord Krishna, as if smiling, spoke these words to the despondent Arjuna in the midst of the two armies.

Once in the land of California in the early 1950s, there was a true avatar. He had come from India in the 20's and his presence was felt on this earth, all around the whole world in one way or another, for he brought a great love.

In another lifetime he had been the mighty warrior Arjuna, whose story had brought to the forefront for every person to heed, the need to fight the battle that rages on

Between good and evil.

Now he had come back again, purely in response to the cries for help,

as Jesus had.

And, he had an answer.

The "As If Smiling" Companion Songs & Commentaries
can be downloaded for free at www.SharonLenoreAnderson.com under the audio books tab

Note: this work has not been acknowledged or endorsed by any institution or person mentioned within it. It is purely the thoughts of the author. Nothing more.

back cover of Kalamalka lake, in the Okanagan Valley: photo done by Kelowna Photografix

AS IF SMILING

by Sharon Anderson

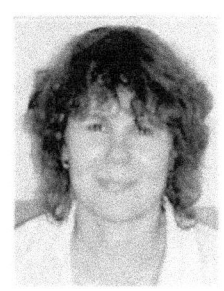

3 BLACKIE	(THE MANY CHAPTERS OF BOBBY CROWELL)
7 THE UGLY DUCKLING	73 MY HELP COMETH
9 JESUS IN THE BROOM CLOSET	77 ELEPHANT IN THE ROOM
15 THE HERO	83 THE WINTER OF OUR DISCONTENT
21 SWAMIJI	89 GIFTED
25 SOMEONE I AM IS WAITING FOR COURAGE	
31 UNCLE	97 DREAM A LITTLE DREAM OF ME
35 THE RIVER OF LIFE	111 YOU'RE IN MY BLOOD LIKE HOLY WINE
43 THOU MIGHTST SEEK IT IN MY ARMS	129 LOVE IS A ROSE
47 THE LEGEND OF GERALD	133 THOU ART THAT
53 COMANCHE	137 OVER THE EDGE
57 HOW GREEN IS MY VALLEY	141 AT LAST IT WILL BE DONE
63 JUST SING	145 GUIDING ARJUNA'S CHARIOT
69 I AM THE ROSE OF SHARON	

sharon_l_anderson@comcast.net

Illustrations by Ollie Anderson
www.sharonlenoreanderson.com

BLACKIE

As I gaze into the eyes of my beautiful guru on my desktop picture, I see more and more into things. For some time now, I have even been brought back to my childhood, and the first time I remember these eyes penetrating into my being. I must have been about 4. It seems from my infancy, I was on a mission to come back. To where I was never sure, but learning how to walk was important to me for this reason. I knew I had a true home to go home to, and I wanted to get back there. Perhaps I had gotten lost and had taken a wrong path somewhere along the line. In any case, here I was again to learn what mistakes I had made.

I was born this time into a hardy robust clan of Paul Bunyon type people; the Quintals. They went their own way and catered to no one .
Supremely loyal they were to family, but if an outsider could cut it, well..they could stay. And inborn within this extended family of cousins, uncles, aunts, inlaws and friends, there was a courageous kind of integrity, and a grand sense of pride and belonging. I sensed I had been chronically lonely in my previous search, and so thrived in this woodland wilderness; this oasis in the middle of the vast prairie that extended up to the Rocky mountains. We lived in a little farming community in Northern Alberta in the mid 50s where the elements could be brutal. The old timers laughingly said our climate consisted of eight months of winter and four months of bad sleddin. It was dangerous, but God watched over the kids especially. And, Yogananda was there. How I drew his protection, I don't know. But it had to be amazingly good karma.

As I was saying, at age 4 or so, I ventured up the hill from home, past the railroad tracks and off I went down the gravel road. It was exciting. I hadn't been noticed, so this would be my first big adventure. My little sister Ollie toddled along behind me, but I didn't pay any attention to her. I was on a mission. Our old black lab "Blackie" ambled warily behind. His job was to guard our store, and he had been there when we had moved in.

It was the Calahoo General Trading store, and our living quarters were in the back of it. He usually did his duty, but this day he was concerned for the safety of two awfully small kids. He was always known to guard us ferociously. One time when we had been playing too close to an oncoming train, he woke up like a shot, attacking the roaring threat, and was thrown bloodied down the hill. It was not surprising then, that he was attending to us now. After about a mile, I came to Patrick's lane. It was a pretty winding road, and it curved around a picturesque pond. I wondered how I could get to the other side. I could see the road over there, but couldn't see how to get there . Then I perceived that the lane had disappeared where the willow branches had obscured the view, so I walked that way, and did finally end up on the other side.

Then to my horror, I saw little Ollie enter the lane. She looked lost, but when she saw me on the other side of the pond, she hurried to reach me, plopping into the pond, immediately over her head. Nothing... I was frozen in fear. Then, like a flash Blackie appeared and lunged into the water. He disappeared too, but then emerged with Ollie's collar in his mouth. My dad's pick up came scooting around the corner, and soon the whole ordeal was over. But, Blackie looked at me deeply. And in that moment, I never forgot his eyes. They were Yogananda's.

Blackie played prominently in my early life. He was a true inspiration. He had already been old when we bought the store, and got much older. Hardly able to walk finally, he would still rally to run off with a pack of dogs for a week or so once or twice a year. Well, Ralph Walker shot at some wild dogs out behind his pig pasture in the dark one night. He was sorrowed to see he had killed our beloved Blackie. I was inconsolable. It wasn't until years later that I realized he had gone out like a warrior.

 Little Ollie grew up to be a quiet strength to me. I was prone to dwelling foolishly in realms of "me, me me" during bewildering times in my life; reverting to habits of blame, complain and obsess. She had integrity even at a young age. She took the brunt of many misfortunes, simply because she didn't bother to speak up for herself.

She had such inner beauty, and it came out in works of exquisite art throughout her childhood and adult life. I am thankful for her, and grateful I got to stay near her.

I loved nature though, and sensed God there. Thus, when I was exploring and playing outside, I was content. The pastures and woods were magic places where I had special spots; little hovels and caves that were my sanctuaries from the world. The sky was my canopy and I thrilled under her vast cover daytime or dead of silent night. I wondered for miles through fields and cow-trails to find any remnants of old homesteads or places where human or animal may have gathered, and then carefully studied how their lives would've been in such places.

How beautiful the world was to me then. Sometimes the grassy ditch beside the railroad track would fill with fresh rain, and there was a railroad tie- plank stretched across it. I would dress down to my undies and jump off this bridge into my refreshing little pond, all the while feeling that angels were giggling and huddling close by. They could take my arms and fairly lift me right off into the sky, like I was their own little pet person. And, gliding across the satiny patchwork quilt of land, I could hear the tinkling breeze and smell the musky fragrance of the moss & ferns that darkened the entrances of the trails leading inward, toward the heart of the woods.

I imagined castles, Indian teepee settlements, leprechaun forests, but mostly just me making my beautiful way home. I could fall asleep in an alfalfa field with its rich aroma, and the gentle hum of God's creation in my ear, while wisps of cottony clouds that got left behind just melted into blue. Stretched out in comfort, I was deeply loved there by some unseen one who had placed me exactly at this spot; protected from the wind's crisp direction by a grainery wall, delicately stroking my face with the suns warming rays.

THE OAK IN THE GARDEN
IS STANDING ALONE
THE FLOWERS HAVE DIED
AND THE SEEDS OF THE PUMKIN
HAVE BURIED THEMSELVES IN THE GROUND
NOT TILL SPRING TO BE FOUND
THE COLDEST TIME OF THE YEAR
AND ONLY A TREE STANDS THERE

ONE LONELY CHILD AM I   LIVING ALONE
THE SEEDS OF A FAMILY BY THE WIND
HAVE BEEN BLOWN TO THE SEA
AND OTHERS HAVE DIED BUT NOT ME
MY ROOTS GROW DEEP IN THIS GARDEN
BUT I AM THE ONLY TREE

AND WHEN I HAVE STOOD HERE
SO STILL FOR SO LONG
WITH THE PAIN OF THE COLDNESS
AND BARE TO THE BONE
A WARM BREEZE RUSHES OVER ME
WHISPERING PROMISE
THIS GARDEN WILL GROW

A WELCOME I'LL BE
FOR THOSE WHO COME HERE TO LIVE WITH ME
AND HUMBLY I CRIED
THAT I HAD NOT DIED

AND WELL SHOULD IT BE
THAT I AM THE
ONLY TREE

(song by sharon)

THE UGLY DUCKLING

Sometimes though, in spite of the beautiful surroundings I could access, I found being here unbearable.

I was an oddball. I was in fantasy too much of the time. When practicality deemed that children be gathered into the corral of normal communal activity, I became painfully aware that I didn't belong. Not at all. Even under the protection of family, I was singled out as nervous, shy and rather bumbling. My cousins had to stick up for me. I became confused and cried at the drop of a hat. Cruelty in the world was especially abrasive to my spirit. I began to lose hope that I would ever fit in. I remember at a crucial stage of low self esteem, I came across a story in my beloved Enchanted Trails books. It was "The Ugly Duckling". I felt so sorry for him. He was just like me. Imagine my delight then when I found out that he got mixed in with the ducks by mistake. He was no duckling but a baby Swan, no less! I squealed in approval. A beautiful baby swan—how wonderful. No wonder he was gawky and acted so differently! I took heart in a big way.

And, I think it was the older Quintal boys who rallied to boost my confidence in those days. I so admired them for their daring and their gallantry. And finally one of those cousins gave me a chance. It was Pug. He would be my mentor in years to come too. So would many of the others after his acceptance of me. A bunch of the older kids were on their bikes storming off very importantly somewhere with a shout. I pedaled urgently to keep up, for they hadn't told me to go back this time. We got to a hill, and I was gasping. The rest of them topped it and were gaining speed. Pug stopped on the crest and quickly glanced back at me. I looked up at him scared. His face softened. He earnestly chirped "Cmon..". I don't think I ever tried so hard. I made that hill and over it I went. I belonged now. I would do my best not to ever fall behind again. I was much more like a swan now, I thought.

My relationship with this particular bird has a wonderful feature. It invites reflections of Master. He was very earnestly moving upward in his journey too when he was a child. So much so, that he not only became a Swami, but later a Paramahansa: a swan. One who was most graceful and regal. This position was named for the swan by the bird's ability to separate water from other liquids in its bill, thus sipping the pure nectar of truth and discarding the delusion. To strive to be a swan had been my great fortune as a little girl. For it led me to learn someday of the grandest Swan I could ever imagine.

Even though at the time it seemed to me that I had gotten mixed in with a different brood by mistake, It was no mistake! It was *because* of my mistakes, rather. This was the very next experience I needed to teach me the next thing I was ready to learn. Weren't we all really baby swans to some developing degree, caught up in the wrong place trying to struggle our way back to our father and our divine mother? Yes, I felt like I finally belonged with this earthly family, but my striving was starting to detour outward, not inward. Detour is the key word, for It assumes getting back on the path before the finish line. We were all being steered toward learning the delusive ways of the world. My innocence would fade as I started school, and incessantly strove to excel in every sport I could find; competing and trying also to attain other goals, all *for* me, *by* me, instead of for *all* by *God*. Master was buried in there somewhere though, waiting ever so patiently for the fruit to ripen. Someday instead of seeing Pug at the top of the hill, I would, deep in meditation, see the face of Swamiji there, like a magnet pulling me up that hill with the most overwhelming love. But we haven't introduced him yet. He comes later. Suffice it to say, that with Master's grace, I was given a savior. He lived right here in the same world at the same time as me, and had been trained by Master. He knew his way intuitively around this battle ground, and wanted to help. It's not so much that he wanted to help me specifically. In fact, he doesn't even really know me. Indeed, still, if I hadn't found his love, my heart would have broken.

JESUS IN THE BROOM CLOSET

So my schooling started in a little 2 room schoolhouse in front of a bigger newer one. Our grade 1 and 2 building had a little pot bellied stove and a bucket of drinking water with a dipper. When we got wet in the snow at recess, Mrs. Ogle would take our trousers and socks off and drape them on a chair close to the stove, while we sat in a towel. I was still enthralled with the love of my special one who watched over me. My heart stayed warm and was reinforced by Mrs. Ogles kindly elderly smile. This was a catholic school, and we would go to church once a month. The whole school would skip off down the main street of Riviere Que Barre, (a dirt road, really..) to a grand cathedral type church with beautiful statues of saints and the virgin Mary holding baby Jesus, placed up high all around a large medieval styled alter. There was an upstairs at the back where the choir sang tones of gracefully flowing ribbons, above the rich surging bellows of a beautiful old pipe organ. There were huge columns that seemed to lead to the clouds, and swirlingly carved old wooden peus . It smelled of purity in there, like the breath of Jesus himself. Seated there we were holy, and my spirit soared, timelessly contented with the saints.

The old priest; father McIntyre was a giant burly man with big freckled hands, red curly hair and plump smiling cheeks on which sat blue twinkling eyes, just like Santa Clause. He smoked a pipe that I have been able to smell in reflection my whole life since his death. He had been a boxer in his younger days, but he was now so very humble and sweet. He would come to the school to take confession, and we would go off by twos to a room where we would sit on his lap and tell him our sins.

My cousin Vickie and I would go in together, and he would smoosh our cheeks with kisses and hug us so tightly, murmuring with delight as we tried to explain what we did wrong. His was an ecstatic childlike affection. He was one of us.

I received my first communion in that grand cathedral, wearing a beautiful little white wedding dress with petticoat and hoopskirt, to give myself in pure love to God. And years later I would kneel there for my confirmation too, in front of Father and an attending bishop. I took the confirmation name of Joan for my patron saint; Joan of Arc, and hoped in my heart I may become brave and die for such a cause as she had.

Jesus however, remained somewhat of a mystery to me. I loved and admired him of course. But I didn't really know him like I knew father Mcintyre. One day in grade 3, after we had moved to the bigger school, I saw my classmate Marietta; a deeply pious farm girl, going into the broom closet at recess. A few of us inquired and found out she prayed in there. She asked if we would like to come in, and there I experienced my comforter. I don't even remember what was said. All I remember is, he was there. Marietta so quietly and lovingly spoke of him, that I didn't know such a state of mind existed. I was entranced.

I squinched my eyes closed and there between them was the clearest path I could find that got up close to him. And there my heart glowed, so that the memory stayed with me to this day. I got to feeling his warmth in my heart out on the playground too, looking off to the horizon in the days and months to come. I started wanting to become a nun like Marietta did.

If most of my fellow human beings had been like Marietta, I might have embraced Jesus' teachings the way they were meant to be experienced. But Master's expression "Environment is stronger than willpower" sadly is too true. Most people in our communities didn't go to church. They didn't talk intimately with Jesus. It seemed more like they treated him like some far off judge whom they could pray stilted verses to when something went wrong. I clung to him for a time. But he started fading. I didn't have the stamina to pray, simply because I didn't equate suffering with being far from Him. I suffered alone.

I tried during the week of Lent, to do the Stations of the Cross at our Calahoo church on my way home from school.

I finally convinced the bus driver to let me off at the church with the older kids, but the rainfall had left the parking lot a muddy mess, and I got stuck and had to be pulled out. I did my Stations, but when I got home I got a lickin from my mom for wrecking my clothes. Still I desired so to please him, and got off again at the church a second day. I again got stuck and again got a lickin. I had heard that one must be persecuted for their belief in God, and we must all carry our own cross, but when I got my third lickin for visiting Jesus (and it was a bad one), I started to think he hadn't noticed me, and got discouraged.

And too, I was starting to be confused about his teachings. How could God send somebody to Heaven or Hell, if they died as an infant or young child? You just couldn't learn or experience enough to have a ready report card by the end if you just hadn't lived long enough.

It made more sense that we come back here again to keep learning. Then, I reasoned, Mozart could have written a symphony at age 4. He already had studied music. ✷

There were contradictions in the Bible too. I had to grow in maturity and in spirit to finally be ready to hear what Yogananda brought to our generation at the behest of Jesus. Finally the pieces of the puzzle would start to fall in place for me. I would learn that Christ had come to the world while it was in a darker age, caused by the orbiting location of our universe at the time. Much higher ages had passed before, when our very universe had been closer to its dual sun core. Right now, as it happens, we are ascending in the orbit and have progressed from an age that was entrenched in concepts of matter, into one that understands energy.

In thousands of years we will progress to conquer the illusions of time and space, to embrace thought transference, and to naturally know our higher selves. Jesus was trying to communicate to those who "had ears to hear and eyes to see". The world, however was, during his time entrenched in a very material existence and couldn't perceive such lofty truths as reincarnation and God consciousness. So he spoke in parables; little idealistic stories. That way at least a sense of decency and right action could be inspired in those who could perceive only the fringes of these truths.

After he was gone, dogmatic thinking began to once again creep into the minds of those grasping to make sense of what he had said, and even his direct references to the truths got left out of the Bible, or watered down in their contexts. Those closest to him had perceived many truths. But after a time, it would only be the saints (in every religion) who, by experiencing God's very consciousness in ecstatic communion, would perceive these truths. And they indeed got persecuted for veering off the trail of the common beliefs of their times.

They knew what was ultimately required of them though, for they were in communion with what they strove to reveal within themselves. Earthly desires and habits would only chain them to the necessity of rebirth. To be settled in the heavenly realms, one needs peace in his heart; stillness, purity of heart, and not wanting for anything that would be left behind after the death of the body. Because they attune themselves to the Masters; who channel the essence of God, they overcome restlessness. They ascend into that more subtle, far more powerful flow. Then higher realms can be achieved. (You invite **yourself** by being able to linger there without being pulled down by your own lower nature, having developed the integrity meticulously throughout your devotional practice. I could describe a drunk trying to sing in the choir. You just can't fit in-- in the state you're in.)

The saints' understanding furthermore, has always been vastly beautiful in its simplicity; unlike complicated dogma. What shone in their hearts was their treasure; God alone, for they knew intuitively Jesus' words;

 "Be ye therefore perfect as your father in Heaven is perfect".(Mathew 5:48)

"The peace and harmony of the heavenly courts will not be marred by the presence of one who is rough or unkind. He who, in this world exalts self in the work given him to do, will never see the kingdom of God unless he is changed in spirit, unless he becomes meek and lowly, revealing the simplicity of a little child" (8T 140)

"If you are to be saints in Heaven, you must first be saints upon the earth "(Timothy1:45)

"The kingdom of God is within you". (Luke 17:21)

We are lucky to be here now, at this time. We can set aside these superfluous rules, and see very far beyond. Now that we are into the age of energy, see how science has found out about the energy at the root of all that is material. Different levels of vibrating energy is all that matter is. And in coming ages, it will become apparent that even that energy is the thought or "word" of God; like a script in the ongoing drama or "play" manifesting from the consciousness of the creator. It is all God's dream.

If I feel badly over having done poorly in a meditation, it is worth considering that the apostles fell asleep during their meditation in the garden, at the apex of their spiritual development with the Master. For, he was to be with them only another day. Think, though, that they were all allowed to see the comforter still. We have come a long way. Take it as Master's blessing when given an interval. Then come back fresh and break down the doors to find him.

*

And too, some unpopular notions at the time Constantine was assembling the bible, *did* happen to get left in the bible cannon unobstructed, and they sure do make sense when considered sensitively. Jesus referred for instance, to John the Baptist as being the prophet Elijah. So, here he was manifest again in another body. The teachings of Jesus and the scriptures tell us "Thou art that", and that we too can "become sons of God". Therefore, you could reason that we would come back too, until we can "sit at the right hand of the father and Go out no more"; Go out into this progressions of lifetimes. Some come back to help like Jesus, Yogananda, Buddah, Krishna, etc. Others may not choose to come back once they are free. After all, "In my father's house there are many mansions."

How Wonderful!

Blue is a color   and beyond the rising of the sea
Is the spirit born in me
A deeper blue   I have learned
Away from you   I have turned
And fell into this dream
You think that I'd know better   you and I are one forever
How far I have come to understand
A prodigal returning I never did stop yearning
To find my way back home again
Was it always in the plan
Love is more now than it was then
Blue is a color   in a sky full of wonder   heavenly
When I knew you lived in me
But I've been blue   and I've been blind
To live in a world   that's in my mind
Oh I can't bear to lose you
You think that I'd know better you and I are one forever
How far I have come to understand
It's only in my soul   that I can come to know
How to be all that I am
You would chase the clouds away   you made it easy
Bringing me a brighter day   free and easy
Blue is just a color..

by cris cuddy, peter cronin, and sharon

THE HERO

Of course, it's no-one's fault that religion got so confusing. The Scriptures and the Bible are themselves products of the age we are in. Higher ages needed no written word, or language for that matter. Those who are here in this age are at this stage of their learning, and dogmatic mistakes will come with the territory. But, oh how blissful to be free. In every age, there are those who yearn deeply for this, no matter which age they got born into. If those beings trying so hard to progress were not here to stir things up a bit, how could the masses see that there *is* a path that actually goes somewhere? They bring great motivation. And, a less enlightened setting for them is fertile ground for progress; less complacency. They came here for a purpose. They become saints.

We are subject to the natural law of attraction, of which gravity is an obvious manifestation. It gets so much more subtle than that, however. To every action there is an equal and opposite reaction. This is karma. What goes up must come down. What goes around comes around. You emote hate, it comes back to you. You give love, you get love. How the currents of karma work time wise is tricky to know. But to know that it is an exacting law, we must. Everything we've done in many lifetimes must be dealt with, and the highs and lows must be neutralized to a calm center, so we can just simply be the ocean of all there is, that is God. Desiring, disliking or even *liking* things in relation to you as a separate entity is not helpful. You are not separate from God. But emotions make you think you are. And, they propel you out into waves of excitement, for example; away from Gods bosom of vast ocean. One small entity like a wave isn't stable. Nor does it posess the power or tranquility of the whole ocean.

For every wave, there's a trough too; a fall as a result of every rise and vise versa; a never ending quagmire in other words.

The continuing of these desires and habits create *more* karma instead of dissolving any.

The vibration of the metronome must cease, and finally rest at the core. Then, peace. Some day the vibration of matter will be no more when we are released from these bodies at death. Best to have the karma neutralized by that time, so that there are no cross currents. You are like a magnet then with all your molecules pointed towards God. You don't necessarily have to work on each individual mistake though. You have rather, effectively corrected your karma by just choosing and cultivating a strong current in the right direction. Meditation , right action, and love can lead you to bliss and your resulting release of karma frees you to rise above the cares of the world's countless act play. Once we are out of delusion, and aware of being part of the ocean of God, we will see that none of the little fluctuations of our lives really changed the surface anyway, from the panoramic view.

If we seek to become aware of our oneness with God in this life, and make an effort towards perfecting that enlightenment, we get closer to the goal of not having to be born in a place like this again to work on any more karma. We will have cleaned it all up. Finally we won't even need our cumbersome bodies. We will know true bliss.

The Avatars like Jesus, Budda, Krishna, Yogananda, come because of the heartbreaking cries for help of those realizing how far they've gotten away from God; the prodigal sons. When we realize how badly we want him, we'll do anything to come back home. Here is an encouragement. This desire is exacting too, within the subtler gravitational laws of attraction. The desire to know God attracts help. (Even the question when pondered thoughtfully "who am I "..where does this 'I' come from when it gets in my thought"; this question must generate an answer when pursued with purpose. And to be lead back to the origin of 'you' means you have achieved an enlightened state. You see yourself in all then.)When worldly life has become an anguishing monotony, The Saviors come-- in all the ages. And, earnest seekers have the potential to become saints in all the ages too. It can be a far climb or a close one, depending how far you've come; just as in meditation, you can be all the way down at the bottom of the chakras in your awareness, but you can still focus steadfastly at the spiritual eye and rise to freedom above God's dream into God.

The closer you get to God, the more childlike you will become. We will awaken to find that we too are dreaming the dream, for "we are that". How to get out of the dream state though, and out of delusion? What does the hero do in the dream play of God?

Does he rescue you and take you to a better world? Ultimately he will take you out of the world completely. How? Well, you wouldn't be able to hear his message in the distracted state you're in, so he comes in off left stage as the 'character' of the hero. All he needs to do is tap you on the shoulder and say "wake up".

If you are tuned in enough to hear that, then you don't ever have to turn back. You're on your way. You have opened your windows to God's grace. Going back then would be like settling for eating mud instead of grapes. "For all those who received him, gave he the power to become sons of God"

"Ye shall know the truth, and the truth shall make you free"   Jesus.   *

Your family are many and prayers they are plenty
for you are a backbone to this body we share
you hurt when we're hurtin and I know for certain
without you life's burden is one I can't bear
--Come to my temple dwell thee within me
I ask for your holy and sweet touch
here to come home to and I'll always love you
my one and only --my Jesus

Faith will grow stronger our fellowship longer
your face growing clearer and closer each day
with every sun sinkin till dawns final twinklin
this melody ling'rin to call me away
--Come to my kingdom dwell thee within me
you've asked for my holy and sweet touch
I'm here to come home to and I'll always love you
your one and only --your Jesus

(song by sharon)

✱ A Page to Ponder

THE WAVE CAN'T SAY IT'S THE OCEAN, BUT THE OCEAN CAN SAY IT'S THE WAVE

Many Christians think that only Jesus can or will free you. He said "No man cometh unto the father but by me". He identified himself in one of two ways in the Bible; son of Man, and Son of God. Speaking of his little self he might say something like "Why callest thou me good? None is good, save one—God." But he was identified also with the Christ Consciousness; the reflection of God in all creation. It was perfectly manifested in him. Thus he sometimes uttered profound comments like "I and my Father are one", or "No man cometh unto the Father but by me". (If you took everything he said literally, then he would be on one hand telling us "Only I can save you", while on the other "But how can I; I'm not even to be called 'good'"..)
A truth cannot be perceived through reason. Only through intuition.. You can't reason what Jesus may have meant. You can develop intuition through the direct experience of truth. This is what you gain access to in meditation and deep prayer. Thus Yogi's can see places that are out of the eye's range and bring forth facts they've never studied in books. Thoughts are universally and not individually rooted. Reason just causes static. Intuition opens the channel up wide and clear. Think of a bottle of ocean water in a container in the ocean. Our reason is the thin membrane that serves as that container. Dissolve it, and we commingle with all that is. Thus Jesus could say that you come to the father through him, because He is in Him; I am in Him, We all dwell in that vast consciousness with all the others of us, for We are in it, of it..We all ARE it. If you or I wake up into that awareness, then we realize nobody can come to the Father except through us as well for we are part of that pool too. We had simply been manifesting a stepped down version of God in our awaren However, he was never different than us; merely more.

Now, if you say you don't intuitively feel that you are part of all that is; the consciousness of God, that will come. Part of the impetus for the unfolding of these perceptions, (or rather the lifting of the veils that have been covering these truths,) comes from seeing an example of something provable.
Do some exploring. Don't simply be a doubter. We didn't think you could contain sound and send it somewhere before the telephone. Then much more was done once that feat was out there to build on.
People didn't think a man could run a mile in four minutes. Once that barrier of realization was broken, we had the spark to do ever better. Consider this; on the 60 Minutes TV show last month, there were several people gathered who had the uncanny ability to recall any day in history they had experienced or known of. They would maybe say what the weather was in a certain place, who was in Office then, whether it was a Tuesday, which sports teams played, and who won, etc. They drew from seemingly unlimited pools of information. It turns out they were all rather particular people; compulsive in their 'records' being orderly, so to speak. To be compulsive for God, and seeking oneness with him is the far better aim. Then too, there are people who draw from information they could not have gained in a worldly way; consider the people who help in Police cases, seeing in their mind's eye a body hidden somewhere they have never been.
There was also a man on the TV show 20-20 a couple years ago, who was very yogic. He stayed under water for 40 minutes. He had dwindled his restlessness to a point of calm, where the body needs to draw no carbon. So, he didn't need to breathe. In this state you can perceive all that is around you because the body, nervous system, senses etc. throw up no barriers. If you lived in proximity to a saint; an awakened person, you would glean much, and with discipline, could attune to that consciousness. Even if you study the histories of many Saints, you would see where they levitated, ate nothing, walked on water, bi-located, etc.
Master has brought people back to life, served a large group from a pitcher of juice less than a third full, etc., but he never did dwell on such things, and considered miracles rather a distraction. Poor Saint Teresa of Avila would clutch her prayer stool, hoping nobody would be distracted by her body floating up when she drifted into ecstatic union with her beloved.
If it hadn't been such a dark age, Jesus might have openly gone into more subtle teachings about the consciousness that reveals your oneness with the Father; your own origin traced back from a prodigal son's folly to your home once again. Saints can realize this awareness in ecstatic communion through prayer, yogis through meditation. Thus "The truth will make you free", "Be ye therefore perfect as your father which is in Heaven is perfect". "The Kingdom of God is within you". Jesus   **Be A Cause -- Not An Effect**

this page is featured as an audio reading on cd at bac

I am the word   so long fortold
when my father claimed me for his own
my time on earth was seven years from 40
when I achieved the task he set before me

Still I pray and seek each face
searching every continent and race
among the fold is where I found my callin
and I will not forsake you where you've fallen

I am here Gethsemene   forever here down on my knees
the bread of life for people here are starvin
I'm Jesus in the garden

All who are lost and call my name
I will find you clean and whole again
when this world is dark and storms are blowin
no need to worry where you're goin

For I am here and here I'll stay
No the cross could not keep me away
Just like the geese a 'comin back a' landin
Till the last of all my sheep are standin

I am here Gethsemene   forever here down on my knees
the bread of life for people here are starvin
I'm Jesus in the garden

(song by sharon)

I put a candle in the window for you
the glow is gentle   the message is true
in a world losing it's way   A candle burns
a power's in play
In the stillness of my heart I can feel
light to revive me   Love that can heal
there's passion in the words you said
a spark of hope   Has started to spread
And flames that are dancing
Yellow Red and Blue
They burn with such a beautiful glow
but something's really alive about the fire i feel for you
it leaves the purest truth in my soul

I put a candle in the window for you
and in my darkest hour   Your face shone through
brighter every breath I take
they say there's no time   But i know there's a way..

song by sharon

SWAMIJI

The first time Swamiji tapped me, I heard him. But, I was enmeshed in the world. I was in my late 20's in the mid 80's and was playing music for a living and writing songs. I thought being famous and having lots of money might be fun, and so I was seeking it. There was a nice side effect to this way of life though. In a world that seemed so rigidly routine and impersonal, I found, as a young adult away from home, that these musicians on the north side in Edmonton were so sweet. They truly loved the music and studied their mentors devotedly. They relished each other's company and helped each other hone their crafts. The music was fresh and inspired, and we felt like we were contributing something wonderful to the world.

My room-mate Ron came back from a trip he had taken to a village in California called Ananda. Our piano player Bow's sister Karen had gone there to live. It was founded by Swami Kriyananda who taught the teachings of his late guru Paramahanse Yogananda. The people there were sensitive, artistic and a little hippyish, like us. Ron brought home 2 books; Autobiography of a Yogi, and The Path, written by Master and Swamiji. He started me on the path of meditation, and showed me the energization exercises Master had created to aid the energy of the body to rise upward in meditation. We started eating healthy and I quit drinking alcohol and smoking. It was so nice. But then I was floored to read this "Autobiography of A Yogi". My life crucially shifted then and there. I knew suddenly that there was so much more to know. As awed as I was, I was also overwhelmed. It was too much to aspire to. My hopes had been realized; there *WAS* something to life. The problem was, I was nowhere in the vicinity of being able to reach for it. I wasn't disciplined and driven enough. I read 'The Path', and took those teachings to heart, as Swamiji was so adept at describing the struggle inherent in seeking truth. No one I knew of had ever tackled this subject, let alone in such a fresh and approachable way. I relished the descriptions of his experiences, and etched them in my mind. For many years to come I would refer to his teachings in 'The Path' to instruct me. Swami Kriyananda and Ananda won a prized spot on the shelf of my highest regard and aspirations.

He had made his mark. Now, he waited.

 I was to go to Nashville next. Not California.

Master, however, met me at the border.

In a year or so, I would be heading for Winnipeg Manitoba; halfway across Canada, to go to our Canadian Country Music week celebration. I had my old brown van filled with everything I owned, as I was planning to move to Nashville after the event. I had gone to work at Whistler Mountain and way up north into the Northwest Territories and the Yukon for many months, to make the money to go on this life altering adventure. This was it. I attended the Music week events, and on the morning I was to cross the border, became wary. Here I was hundreds of miles from home, and all alone, going into a new country. I had been advised during the week, that you couldn't move to the USA, and needed a visa to work there. Leaving Winnepeg through her downtown area, I rounded a corner, where Master appeared in my mind suddenly, and I had to see him. I needed his book. I needed it in my hand. I looked quickly down the street on the left, and my eyes fell on a book store sign. I found parking. I went straight in, down a few rows, turned right, and saw the Autobiography of a Yogi, with his beautiful face. I quickly bought the book. Now, with him sitting on the seat beside me, I could cross the border. I approached the gate, and a man came out to speak with me. "What are all these amps and speakers for?"

 "I want to learn to be a good songwriter" I said.

"Do you plan to work there?"

"I plan to study songwriting" I said, " by writing songs with people who know how."

" What do you need the gear for then?"

" To record demos of the songs I write."

" Why do you have so much stuff?"
" It might take a long time" I said.
"Are you living down there?"
" I have no place to live. I have money, with which to stay in motels or pay room and board."

The guy kind of shrugged. He had a row of eighteen wheelers behind me to tend to. "Alright" he said. I drove through. Talking to one of the truckers about maybe going through Chicago as the best route, he asked a few questions of me and commented; "It's a miracle you got through. He should never have let you, according to the rules."

remember that older girl walked you home from school
when you missed your ride
and she said that it was on her way when it was really a 2 mile hike

there are people everywhere   you don't even realize
doing the work of God on earth   living quiet lives

and I hope you know that I love you
and there's no need to ever be scared
when the world gets dark all around you
I will hear your prayer
and there's such a thing as forever
beyond the clouds the sky is forever blue
and I'd lasso the sun and moon to
light the way for you

I knew you in your mama's arms   I've always been a heartbeat away
and while you struggled to get the message clear
I"ve been proud of the choices you've made

there's a spirit stirring in the wind   a power that the world can't deny
when a child of God finally comes of age   forever's in your eyes

and I hope you know that I love you
and there's no need to ever be scared
when the world gets dark all around you
I will hear your prayer
and there's such a thing as forever
beyond the clouds the sky is forever blue
and I would move the sun and moon to
light the way for you

by sharon and Rick Ferrell

When in the cellar of affliction, I look for the Lords choicest wines..
samuel rutherford

It is an amazing thing to look back and fit together the pieces of my spiritual puzzle. To see Master, for instance—at age 4. Those early years were especially endearing as I remember again, in wonderment..

Sometime along when grade 2 started in the little school, my uncle Shmoe's family had gone away to Ontario on the pipeline and my cousin Vickie was gone. I had been raised with her for a time as an infant when my own mom and dad had gone on a pipeline job, and I grew to think Vickie was a part of me. I collapsed without her at school and at home, and fell into a pool of depression. My mom didn't know what to do with me. My grade 2 teacher, however; Miss Dew took me on with great love, trying to bring my spirit out into the sunshine. And, the dew of grace in a brand new morning is what she finally became, as I started to try in every way to please her. I remember a trip to the big Namao school for a lavish concert our school was part of. Under Miss Dew's guidance, I became part of the performance offering of the lower grades, and I had a carefully rehearsed poem to deliver on that big stage in front of the many schools in the division. I don't know how I had the courage to do this. I only remember I did. I stepped out on the stage all by myself and looked out into the vast room, feeling only one set of eyes on me. Lahiri. I wouldn't know who he was until much later. His spirit was beautifully flickering in the room and like a father, he was tenderly caressing me with courage. He had, in another life, been the sensitive and beautifully artistic mystic poet; Kabir. I delivered my offering articulately and with love, to him.

UNDER a toadstool crept a wee Elf,
Out of the rain to shelter himself.
Under the toadstool, sound asleep,
Sat a big Dormouse all in a heap.
Trembled the wee Elf, frightened and yet
Fearing to fly away lest he get wet.
To the next shelter—maybe a mile!

Sudden the wee Elf smiled a wee smile.
Tugged till the toadstool toppled in two.
Holding it over him, gaily he flew.
Soon he was safe home, dry as could be.
Soon woke the Dormouse—"Good gracious me
"Where is my toadstool?" loud he lamented.
—And that's how umbrellas first were invented

Oliver Herford. 1863

I went on to win the book award in grade 2 for the most advanced student, and was given "The King's Stilts" by Dr. Seuss, signed lovingly by Miss Dew. I look now at the words of my delivered nursry rhyme poem and a warm thrill flows over me, thinking how they brim with integrity and ingenuity. How clever and wise this little elf was to stand on his own 2 little feet. I too will use my umbrella. He is always there for me.

Lahiri Mahasaya is the guru of Master's guru; his "grampa" guru..we get to meet hi

SOMEONE I AM IS WAITING FOR COURAGE

THE ONE I WANT   THE ONE I WILL BECOME WILL CATCH ME

SO LET ME FALL   (lyric sung by josh groban)
by James Corcoran & Jutras Benoit

One day when I was about 9, I was playing at an abandoned house near our place with a neighbor girl. My little brother Aaron was only about 2 then, and he was there too, standing on the old front porch stoop. A great buzzing started and suddenly I heard a piercing cry and turned to see a swarm of hornets buzzing all around his head. Again and again he jerked with each sting; screaming in agony, his little arms reaching out to me. I was horrified with fear and stood paralyzed in the yard. I kept trying to run to him, but just couldn't.

Then I saw a streak down the road in my peripheral vision, and into the yard ran Ollie, up onto the stoop and grabbed him up into her arms, pulling him out of the swarm. Later that evening my baby brother smiled up at me with a face so swollen, I couldn't see his eyes. I ran to my room and cried miserably, heart wrenchingly, for hours. This was perhaps the first time I knew there was a big flaw in me. I was so disgusted with myself, I could hardly bear it. After that incident, I was never to be the carefree little spirit I had been.. To this day, I am dogged with the nagging awareness that I am a coward.

....

Then there I am, like a wild Indian streaking through Labonte's field flat out at a full gallop .Lurched forward haplessly on the bare back of my horse with arms and legs stretched outward to the sky, I am connected to her by only a wisp of trust, in direct defiance of any cowardly currents that may be trying to cling to me. And relief sweeps over me with the hard wind on my face. In the precarious position, I could be flung to my demise at any slight swerve. But I know my pony, and she seeks to please me. She is steady and strong. Besides, I know this field and have missed all the gopher hole areas.

And so, I determinately make my way up the spine in the silence of my meditation. Thank you Dear Sir, for showing me how to replenish my energy. I now re-focus it ever more deeply back to you, now that I'm back.

> I SAID I'M SORRY   I WAS SO ASHAMED
>
> BUT IT WOULDN'T GET BEHIND ME   EVEN THOUGH I TOOK THE BLAME
>
> SO I LOOKED INSIDE   TO SEE WHAT I COULD DO
>
> AND IT SCARED ME   THE PAIN I'VE BEEN LIVING THROUGH
>
> MY HEART WAS LONELY   IT WAS FRAIL AND THIN
>
> THERE WAS NOTHING THERE TO FEED IT   NO LIGHT WAS GETTING IN
>
> AND I CRIED LORD HELP ME   LOOK WHAT I HAVE DONE TO ME
>
> AS I LAY MY BURDEN DOWN AT HIS FEET
>
> PEACE RIVER ROLLS THROUGH THE HEART OF THE PRAIRIE
>
> CAREFREE WIND SOFTENS THE MEMORY
>
> SOOTHING SKY SPREADS FROM EAST TO WEST
>
> AND SURROUNDS ME IN THE VALLEY OF FORGIVENESS
>
> .... TO FEEL THE SUNS LIGHT   HOW BEAUTIFUL IT IS
>
> SURROUNDED -- IN THE VALLEY OF FORGIVENESS   (excerpt of song by Sharon)

I don't mean to let these memories into my meditation. But, let it come..it already came, so I'll use it. It can be a good practice to will yourself somewhere instantly. From a memory, back to God—lickety split. It may help you some day when you're in a tight spot. Beam me up Scotty.. Think of how it will help should the moment of death come quickly amidst confusing circumstances.

Yes Lord, you have helped me to come back on to the spinepath countless times. Why, at the end of this field, on Labonte's farm, you delivered me into the high realms. That too happened after a suffering. My experiences in life keep telling me I need suffering. I wonder about that, especially after reading accounts of great women saints of the early centuries who relished their sufferings so dearly. Master brought a teaching in this age that encourages us to seek joy in the calm acceptance of things the way they are.

That attitude creates an all encompassing flow of healing energy, devouring our past karmas with its powerful upward surging force. Why suffering then? Well, for those of us who haven't really harnessed the usefulness of that calm acceptance, suffering works too; barbaric though it be.

Consider the boy in the slums who doesn't have a nice environment and sees misery all around him. If he gets a hold of an old motor, he'll try to get it going, put it on a chassy, and get himself out, somewhere nice. He'll work on that motor, tuning it, priming it over and over to get it started, until at last he hears that perfectly pitched whirring hum of success. But a boy who is in a nice neighborhood has lots of other distractions. He will never think of learning how to get a motor running. The boy who tries, will also feel the motor in his heart kick in after so much priming and practice in meditation, having concentrated all the harder, and pleaded incessantly with God to take him up out of his surroundings into the arms of love.

Suffering brings you into the now; the only portal that can lead to God. However, someone who has spent lifetimes looking for God, after having suffered in the beginning, may find himself in this life with some conveniences as a result of the good karma from his searching efforts. Instead of distracting him, then, he uses his free time and peaceful surroundings to facilitate his ongoing search. In this way he too is well motivated, and isn't prone to dwelling in the past or future. Many people here now aren't that focused.

   I'm trying to learn the subtlties of this age of energy, but for much of this life, it was each anguishing instance of suffering that served to intuitively bring me closer to the only thing that can dispel it; love.

One day Lucille Labonte; one of my very best friends, her little brother Squeaky and I, were out in the barnyard. Many times the cold of the Alberta Prairie has prompted me into a dangerous predicament owing to the naivety of my age. Today was such a day. It was cold outside. And, being we were never so discouraged from our outside play, there we were in the barnyard. We got into a grainery thinking it would be warmer in there, at least sheltered from the cutting wind.

There was straw on the floor, and a pail in the middle of the floor. "Why don't we make a fire?" One of us had a match (could it be we had been smoking out behind the barn..having these matches??). Gathering up some of the straw and placing it in the pail, we lit it. It very soon became a monster, our little fire. It got too big and hot to go near, and started spreading to the straw outside the pail. We couldn't see for smoke, and I couldn't breathe. We tried the door, but amazingly, it had somehow been locked or jarred. We couldn't get out. Lucille and I climbed up into the rafters but as far as I remember, poor Squeaky stayed down on the floor. I found a crack between the wood boards near the roof, and formed my lips into a sucking whistle to try and get some air. This is the very spot I find myself in meditation when I just can't get my breath going right. It's like I'm sinking away from God. I..just…can't make it. There is mounting anxiety. I have nowhere to go. Father!! And, there you are. You would never leave me.

Lucille's dad had come into the barnyard inexplicably. How would he have done that just then?

He banged the door open.

And I enter into the top room effortlessly. What a relief. Swamiji you are here, all is well. What was all the fuss about?

And how did I get here into the higher realms after so much distress? Well, my meditation wasn't goIng very well, so I finally surrendered that route. How else can I get there? Necessity is the mother of invention. Relax, so the building's on fire. I might die. That doesn't mean I should give up on my meeting with Swamiji this morning. That would make my day not very bright, would it.. No, I gotta find where he is. Not only that, but I'm sure he's counting on me to be there. If I'm not there he will miss the bliss that comes from my direction. I couldn't have that. So, the breathing will have to not be the focus. I'll sneak upward while just doing the best breath I can, and just peek around. Surely I can get a glimpse of him at least, and he'll know I tried.

Before long I'm drifting up and down pleasantly, feeling the magnetism developing. And presently I find the spot where everybody is.

Let me make clear at the outset here. I speak very devotedly about Swami Kriyananda. Decidedly so, as I think of him as my guru and I have carefully developed and refined my love, as is taught to do. In the sanctuary of my heart I humbly gave him my unconditional love and obedience. I however, don't know if I am even ready for a guru. On some level, I don't even presume that I have attracted one. That happens only to advanced disciples. I only know how I long for it. I accepted Yogananda as my guru in my ceremony, like all the followers of this path have. And, I carefully look into his eyes to read his acceptance of any issue. He condones this, in fact nudges me towards Swamiji, most convincingly at times.

Swamiji's lucid videoed face is the face I have carefully studied thousands of times. His voice is the one I thrill to. I delicately study his words and writings and try to follow his way. I relate so closely to so many of his life experiences. I try to write music like his. He is, in my eyes, the perfect extension of Master. He can access me in the here and now should he choose to; personally, and also impersonally through my daily exposure to his public direction (which can offer very personal answers if one is paying attention). He knows exactly what Master needs to tell me and can deliver it. And, I have felt encouragement to secretly (if need be) attune myself to him, after hearing the story in the Mahabharata about Eklavya, who studied under Drona, even though it was unbeknownst to Drona. Eklavya was not taken into the fold as a student. In fact, he was denied. But, he attuned to this peerless teacher from where he was on the periphery, and learned deeply. Such was the deep yearning of the student to glean from that great one. And I feel that yearning too.

Back in my world of bookblocks and the Ananda website at work, I find Swamiji talking on the anniversary of his finding Yogananda, and this most incredible utterance, it seems just for me and the cowardice that haunts me.

Swamiji said that when a bone is broken, the one that grows in to fix the break is even stronger . When he was a doubter in previous lifetimes, it was the most miserable suffering you could imagine. This lifetime his faith; the opposite of that conquered doubt, is now his strongest attribute.

So, the greatest gift one could have **is** the weakness that will lead to the opposite strength that you find most worthy. Oh Swamiji, you couldn't have told me anything more encouraging. I may be a coward. It seems the worse thing possible, but it means I will be a mighty warrior for truth, like Arjuna, like William the Conqueror, like the great Yogananda, like you, brave Swami Kriyananda. Oh, I want so much to help us all. I want so very much to change. It isn't brave to beat up on your little sister, and that's what I used to do to Ollie. I was bigger, and much more athletic. I have so many shames to get past. Sometimes it so overwhelms me that I have no idea how or where to start. I am happy for her that she is the one who deserves respect, and I respect her so much. My little sister Ollie did a running swan dive off the Athens Tower in the Kelowna city park one day. I happened to see it. She didn't even mention it. And I was always the proud one. Have I improved myself with age, now that I'm grown?

Recently I was riding my bike and a big German Sheppard dog was loose. Oh, I have become brave alright. I even held my head up bravely thinking "this road is my territory, not yours" when I heard his aggressive bark. Well, he promptly caught my drift and came out and bit my leg. Then on the way back down, I tried to show him love, and slowed down to talk to him. He bit me again. My bravery hit the gutter, and I got home shaking like a rabbit. To this day, I am so afraid of that dog, I only have to hear him bark from my driveway, and I shrink. Brave then? I can't let myself be discouraged over and over again this way. Fear is a powerful adversary.

> Sometimes when I'm mentally chanting aum through the chakras, visiting each one, I place the chakra I'm at up into the spiritual eye area, and then aim at it like I was skeet shooting. This is great for getting a lazer like focus on the fly. Your aim gets pretty good. Then, however, I think of the gun as a water squirt gun and get a good flow going, dissolving that skeet, and finally getting the stream flowing right through, briskly and tingly.

UNCLE

So, I do what I can. I'm brave enough to do my meditations 3 times a day, my energization exercises 5 times a week, and try my level best to make progress on my path. And I say "don't worry Sharon (like I was witnessing her from the in side) I'll try to help you".

I think of the people I've been raised with, and take courage. There was my uncle Black who, like other of my uncles was a pipe-liner and had braved the North Country Tundra to build the illustrious steel channel carrying within it a great flow reaching all the folks who could benefit from the newfound gas technology. These uncles were also among the pioneer types who built the great Alaska hi-way.

There was something in the way my uncle Black called me "my-girl" that knitted me into his web of protection with such warmth. But it was also his demeanor, his sun parched face, his mischievious grin, and that certain air of confidence that whisked around him enchantedly. He challenged whatever came in life. And he was a bullet, no matter what angle he got shot from. But he was kind to people. Therein lay his strength.

A few years ago I made a trip back home to Canada with my kids. It had been such a long time. Into the old folks home we went with my aunty Bun to see her brother; my uncle Blackie and aunty Mary. I hugged his neck and began to weep at his greeting.. so much so that I was shaking.

We had a wonderful visit. He told us his stories with the greatest of gusto. When we walked out of the lobby, I made that wistful turn of the head one last time, and there was that face. I took a snapshot of him with my mind. On the way home aunty Bun asked "What did he whisper to you that made you cry like that"?

"I thought I'd never see you again".

I LIVED NEAR A MEADOW WHEN I WAS LITTLE

AND I HAD AN UNCLE   ON THE OTHER SIDE

THE MEADOW WAS YELLOW   TROUBLES WERE SHALLOW

JUST LIKE THE PUDDLES OF RAIN LEFT BEHIND

BY THE TIME I GOT HOME THEY WERE GONE--

AND I KNOW A SECRET NOT EVERYONE DOES

HE WAS PAUL BUNYAN   AND HE HAD NO OXEN

BUT EVERY SO OFTEN   I SAW WHO HE WAS--

TIME SURE HAS TAKEN   TO OUR LITTLE TOWN

WRESSLED ADVENTURE   AND SETTLED IT DOWN

EVERYONE'S SAD CAUSE   THEY'VE HEARD THAT HE'S LEFT US

BUT I KNOW THE SECRET AND I KNOW THEY'RE WRONG

CAUSE I WAKE UP JUST BEFORE DAWN--

WHEN EVERYTHING'S QUIET   THE LEAVES START TO TUMBLE

THE CLOSER I LISTEN   THE MORE IT'S A RUMBLE

AND THERE IN A BLINK   THROUGH A GLEAM IN MY EYE

A GIANT BLUE OXEN   ROARS OUT   CROSS THE SKY

song by sharon

God was playing his life dream game
and in the joy we got propelled out
into existence. He would call us back, if he
* hadn't given us the same freedom of will he*
enjoys. Sadly, we wondered out too far to retrace
* our footsteps, and we're sinking in the maya.*
But, he did leave a loop hole to try and help with
* our rescue; We don't have to play.*
Just stay still, and I will find you, he says. If you don't thrash
around, then you won't sink any deeper, and
* there's a chance I can reach you. Don't cry. Be brave.*
Don't play the game. So you say "I won't play!
* These are all toys I don't need, and desires that are*
useless to me. They are only distracting me. I must
* pay attention so when Father comes, I can reach for him.*
*   I only want father.*
I will not be tempted to play this game, but start to
* work my way back now.*

When I work to loosen the kundalini from karma vrities at the chakras during meditation, I sometimes take to heart that in the Bhagavad Gita, kundalini was characterized as the wife of all the Pondova brothers who fought for good. I think of this kundalini wife then, visiting all her husbands, from the bottom up. She stops at each one, lovingly helping him to prepare for that day's battle with all the mental citizens he will have to deal with. She blesses him with her warm attention, and as he is gently awakened he is refreshed.

She then is able to move up and help her next husband. Sometimes he will be especially happy she is there and they will dwell together contented for a longer time. If the meditation is lacking energy though, and she cannot maintain the attention of her husband, then she must be more like his mother. She must grasp the squirming child and hold him for his blessing, for she doesn't want him to have to pass this day without it!

There was a story in my Enchanted Trails books, that was very scary for me. Little goats being chased by a wolf ran into a house to hide. They were under chairs, tables, in closets, etc. One clever little goat, however, found the perfect hiding place; inside the central giant clock where the door was disguised as a wooden panel. It was terrifying then, as I related to the clever little goat hiding there, to hear all his brothers and sisters being captured and eaten up. I thought in the recesses of my mind throughout my life, that that little goat had been the lucky one. Now I'm not so sure. As it relates to my bee story, for example; he would always have to contend with those bees and be in hiding; never to actually confront them. The others got caught as in a game. It was over, and they got to move ahead. This story also relates to my perception of the kundalini wife. This little clever goat has been hiding from his blessing. And, in such a devious hiding place. He is like the child in the throat chakra, where the medulla is. For some reason, this child has been hard to capture to give his blessing to. It is because he is the ego. Not only that, he is hiding behind time. He will never be free there. I must take special care to visit that chakra with the most tender patience. Yes, that little goat is clever. But, when I have caught him, I will indeed make progress. For when he is free, the devotee will speedily come to thee.

So, this morning I stopped at that chakra. It is not so good to be clever, I thought. You are too good at hiding in there. I paused, and then softly whispered, "If you love me, you have to set me free. Think of the countless lives you have done it your way. Nothing worked. Let Sharon be the one to set me free. Just step aside. You have had your time. If you surrender, you will be happy. You will see. Swamiji says you are the one who is so important in this process. Like the **Voyager** that needed to explore the far reaches beyond Jupiter. The ego possesses power built up from our lower natures, perched to be lifted in realization, refined, and utterly transformed within the magnetism the craft harnessed by circling Saturn fast enough to sling it out into the vast reaches. Please sling me loose.

Your love on my side means everything.

THE RIVER OF LIFE

An endless expanse of pure white light with tiny blue twinkles sprinkled on it. That's what it looked like out the window of our kitchen, past the fields, tracks and out towards Blacks lake. In the wintertime when there were fresh shrouds of snow, sometimes it would get to be four feet or more. Then it covered the fence lines and you were free. All the land became a blanket of white, and there was nowhere you couldn't go on your ski-doo. Places you would never get to see, like river beds, canyon bottoms, and thick bush, were carpeted with powder that called you to come explore there. The gravel roads were packed a little for local traffic, but easy to cross. Bands of merry rosy cheeked villagers would ride to Onoway or Villeneuve through the fields unhindered, to have a hot chocolate at Johnny's Cafe and compare notes on their adventures getting there. Boots would be thawing out by the heaters and there were wet puddles all over the floor. The kids would ride toboggans hitched to the backs of the snowmobiles, and there were snowdrifts that rose like cottony mountains for climbing when the group would stop to taste the still sunlight, nested in a gulley, below the crispy light breezes swirling by.

We liked to go skating at night sometimes. We had a rink with a little clubhouse perched by the gates, and a pot bellied stove inside that we needed to keep stoked. We even had a streetlight built at the rink, and at night would glide in the silence with our tongues out catching big flakes of snow. We had a record player and could hear music as we skated. This was the first time we felt the conditions were right to hold a boys hand. You know, to help hold you up. (Never mind you could play hockey like a banshee) And, first loves blossomed there. The girls would tell their secrets to each other, and I expect the boys would too. Playing games like pum-pum-poloway, capture, and crack the whip, were such fun. Especially when your own special one would pursue you and throw you into the dungeon. He must really like you!

But the greatest adventure of all was what you could do if a hard freeze came before a snow. That meant the Sturgeon river froze

-at least the parts that didn't have beaver dams; those never froze completely. At the farm we had a skating shack; kind of a tree house all rickety, with a make shift stove in it. We would gather there to skate. You had to portage by land around the beaver dams, unless you were brave enough for the leap across, but sometimes we got so caught up in gliding down that river, that we would go 10 miles all the way to Rothweiler's bridge and do just that. It was just too irresistible; around every corner was a new scene; a new secret place the river had to show us, where it would wind its way intricately through groves of evergreens or willows, or stretched itself out triumphantly across a field. We felt like Jaques Cartier exploring the great northern wilderness.

One day about 8 of us headed out on such a journey. Leaving the shack, we were a little timid at first. New territory was beautiful to see, but somewhat alien to us. The first beaver dam took us by surprise. Peter and Crockett, the older boys jumped over it. Peter sailed like a gull, and landed so lightly we barely heard a sound. That gave everybody a spark of courage. But, Linda, then Mooksie broke through as they came close to the dam and got their feet wet. We decided to portage up the bank, partway through the meadow and meet the river up a ways past the next curve. Once together again, off we all went happily. Everybody took their turns at finding water though, and our feet began to get cold. They say God watches over fools and kids, and I imagine he was busy trailing us quite a bit of the time. I went to jump up to the bank and the ice was very thin there. But, it was a lot deeper than you would think. Down I went. I was almost to my knees when I grabbed a branch hanging out above my head. One of the others grabbed me around my waste from the bank and scooted me up onto the ground. The day wore on, and we were getting mightier and stronger, wilier and more clever, braver and more reckless. Peter and Crockett were fairly flying over the beaver dams, and sometimes you could hear a big crack on their landings, and see a crooked line form on the ice. But there was lots of yippin and yahooin. We dove into the day headlong without really feeling the cold of our wet feet.

Then came the mother of all the beaver dams. She was a big one, and there was free water standing on both sides of her. We all headed to the sides for the portage, but Peter prepared to jump. With a big grin he strode out. He sailed really high, but came down with a funny sounding crack as a triangle of ice broke out from beneath him. He went under, and it seemed like slow motion for a moment. But Crocket was already busy. "Get a log" he shouted as he leapt to the shore and quickly found a long tree trunk that had broken. We got another log to him and he tried to get closer to Peter who, by this time was looking kinda scared. He was paddling, but every time he came close to the ice to get up, it broke. Crocket pushed the two poles out on either side of him. Then, standing on both with each skate, he carefully started straddling the rails out to Peter. But wouldn't you know it, when Peter went to grab his hand, the logs slid outward from each other and split Crockett's legs out from under him. Crockett went down too. What an awful sunken feeling I had in my gut. We all fell silent, and then spooked, started babbling helplessly. There was a frenzy of paddling before the boys got a hold of their senses, and grasped the logs, slowly inching them farther along the ice, breaking it along, until they finally got to shallow enough water by a beach-like part of the right bank .

Soon it was getting dark, and we had a sharp reminder of the weather, as we realized we had another 10 miles to go now to get back. We were a team though, and we made it home bloodied, but not broken.

These days my thoughts are more centered, and I have matured spiritually so much. That river has taken on a life of its own within me. It's there that my heart can soar. Sometimes in meditation I can stop at those beaver dams. When I'm calm and happy yes, I can stop there and carefully separate the sticks until a little trickle through starts to form. Other times I hurry by, nervous of the fall I know could happen there. Each one has a hole beneath that, there's no real way of knowing the deepness and intricacies of.

I've got karma bound up in each one of those dams. But Swamiji, aren't you Peter, who sails on through up the spine, leading us ever toward freedom from the river altogether.

Yes, if Yogananda be Jesus, you would indeed be someone like Peter. Although, Peter never showed the gift for the written word you possess, or the talent for crafting beautiful music (like King David). He was, however praised by the Master to be the cornerstone of the work. Yes, Dear Swamiji, we would follow you, though the river be unknown and the dams be great. You have inspired us so intensely with your big grins and wild soaring leaps. Even now dear sir, so late in your current incarnation, you are stirring things up. You have recently taken on a watery dam and have fallen into the drink. But, isn't that your design sir? I see the twinkle in the eye of your picture on my desk. Didn't even Jesus take a fall to serve as a catalyst for larger concepts to enter the scene? The comforter came. * What you have done is to declare a judgment of dis-service on Master's remaining high profile disciple;Faye. She has not been **representing Master's ideals as** head of the organization he founded. Taking your fall meant breaking through the ice for us to see who Master really is. We are all gazing in awe while the truth shines supremely in the moment. He is love. Nothing less. When Peter broke through the ice, he was able to answer Jesus; "You are the Christ".

You are saving Master, even though not everybody can really get a handle on all of it yet. We are, however, 100 percent behind you. And this morning instead of tackling my sections of river in their order, I surpassed it completely, lifting off like a fighter jet in formation with my gurubais behind you sir. Now, with the river below we have leveled out above it all, with only your pole star streaming ahead, and suddenly there are no obstacles. Master said Jesus was crucified once but his teachings have been crucified every day since. I see that won't happen to Master, not on your watch. The gift of truth brought to us cannot be other than the Second coming of Christ, for truth is truth. Jesus could bring nothing different than what is being offered by the coming of Yogananda. And, right action is essential for wrongs to be righted! Master thinks through you, and so is calling for mistakes to be rectified. But so much more than that, he is allowing great opportunities at this late hour, for the redemption of his own.

The time is ripe while his right hand man is yet here to do his bidding. Your work is being tested just as his was toward the end.

But, such beauty in the plot Sir. My hat is off to you. For all of us; your followers, who have grown attached to you in a worldly way, you are martyring your standing. At the very least you are leaving it vulnerable, as if hanging off a cliff. After guiding us to the summit, you are stepping aside into a mesh of temporary maya, to let us see our sovereign God straight ahead, with nothing but our higher selves to cling to. And when it's all over, we can laugh together and say "Great show, wasn't it wonderful!" We all got home. Peter too!

> THERE'S A RIVER SO DEEP AND WIDE   I'VE NEVER SEEN THE OTHER SIDE
>
> BUT I'VE WALKED DOWN BY THE SHORELINE AND I'VE WONDERED   ALL OF MY LIFE
>
> CAN I CROSS OVER AND SEE YOUR FACE   WHERE EVERY HEARTACHE WILL BE   ERASED
>
> OH I FEEL LIKE I COULD REACH OUT AND TOUCH   HEAVEN'Y LOVE...
>
> HERE I AM AND THERE YOU ARE
>
> I WANA MAKE IT WITH ALL MY HEART
>
> I'M NOT GIVING UP   I'M READY TO TOUCH   HEAVENLY LOVE...
>
> I AM A PILGRIM   PASSING THROUGH
>
> MY JOURNEY'S INWARD   CLOSER TO YOU
>
> FOR IN THE TWINKLING OF AN EYE IT WILL BE OVER   AND WE'LL FACE THE TRUTH
>
> OH DID WE MELT THESE HEARTS OF STONE   ARE WE AS CHILDREN BEFORE YOUR   THRONE
>
> SIR, YOU'D DIE TO LET OUR FATHER REACH US   WITH HEAVENLY LOVE...
>
> HERE I AM AND THERE YOU ARE
>
> I WANA MAKE IT WITH ALL MY HEART
>
> I'M NOT GIVING UP   TILL I FEEL THE TOUCH   OF HEAVENLY LOVE

(song by Sharon)

Dear Sir, your love for Master is so complete. It reminds me of your story of Saint Antony of the desert. SRF; the 'Organization' is like the Christian church of that time. They were trying to channel the great Master, but his truths were getting clogged in the line. They were losing the battle of trying to embody that essence of Love and Oneness with all that is-- that he was. And, the confused masses were starting to think of him as human, and not divine. You are a natural conduit for his very thoughts, and the only one who could unclog the stoppage. Such was Antony when he came to their aid, stood up amidst the clamoring argument, and simply stated "I HAVE SEEN HIM".

*Master said the Avatars come again and again. Not always such high profile visits of course; Jesus had been Elisha, Krishna came back as Babaji, and so on. Master said their will to help is unending, and they return. When asked if he was Jesus returning, Yogananda simply redirected saying "would it matter?" But he called his mission the Second coming of Christ. Master lovingly turned to Jesus, attuning his conciousness to that great Galilean master, while writing his interpretations of Jesus' teachings in the Bible. He knew it was at the behest of Jesus that he was sent on this Mission at this time, and he sought to clarify the misconceptions people had formed that skewed the teachings with dogma and confusion. Jesus had told Babaji that his followers do good works but that they had lost contact with him. Thus, he gave Master his glowing approval during one of these attunements; When Yogananda once prayed to Jesus Christ for reassurance that he was interpreting the Gospels correctly, Jesus appeared to him in a vision, along with the Holy Grail, and the Grail passed from his lips to Yogananda's. Jesus then spoke the following words of heavenly assurance: "The cup from which I drink, thou dost drink." Yogananda also saught to bring clarity to the eastern teachings; notably the Bhagavad Gita. He is directing this age toward a unity of east and west to finally embrace the truth that nomatter which side you scale the mountain, it is the oneGod you reach.

Recently, it has been Swamiji's desire that people know what a
generous loving heart was the Master's. I am so happy here to
bring to mind, and let you know of one of my latest dreams of him.
When my daughter Emily was a baby, she was so loving and
dear, as she is now. So soft and comfortable she was to hold,
and she used to spread across my abdomen, somehow fitting up
in there perfectly, with her little arms and legs stratling my core,
hugging tightly. Well, in my dream of Master, I embraced him in
this way, at his invitation. It was like I was his dear baby. Then he
lovingly set me down, and as he was speaking, reached over to
pat me on the head a couple of times.

It doesn't seem so long ago
we all lived in one place
and strangers all were welcome
if you cut it you could stay
& some by heart & some by blood
but boy that family grew
standing up for one another
and we got that from you
--There were horses to be broken then
and pipelines to be built
there were those who worked beside you
who tell their stories still
of wild ways and good old days
the best they ever knew
& they say it with that sideways grin
and they got that from you
--So lets raise a glass & drink a toast
this is your night to shine
these folks are here to celebrate
a true one of a kind
the younger generation learned
one thing you never do
that's miss a chance in life to dance
and we got that from you
as for me - i'm lucky that
i learned to sing the songs
that take me back to times i love
and places i belonged
they let me tell you this with love
and mom would say it too
thank you for the music PeeWee
we got that from you

We are gathered here together
in the fellowship of love
children with their faces glowing
straightly growing up
and families with their heads bowed down
in humble grace renewed
born again to God the father
and they got that from you
--There are stories of the seas that parted
and prophets that became
guiding forces for the people
hero's of their day
& wisdom of the ages told
in parables of truth
For those who heard go spread the word
and they got that from you
So lets raise the cup and lift the bread
this is your time to shine
these folks are here to celebrate
a true one of a kind
Every generation by your body and your blood
know the taste of freedom
and the victory of love
As for me -i'm thankful that
i turned to you in time
to feel my spirit soaring and to
know that God is mine
He called me by my name and all my sins
he saw right through
with a sacrifice for my salvation
And i got that from You..

(song for uncle Peewee that became also a song for Jesus, by sharon)

One time when I was in my early 20's, I was playing up **above the Peace River Valley, near the NWT and** Yukon borders. **It was** a little farming community called Hythe, **north of** Grand Prairie.

There was a man in the lounge who was speaking boisterously, and had everybody happy. I played into the spirit and with the music, we were having a nice little party. After noting his mannerisms , something suddenly occurred to me, and from the stage I announced "You know PeeWee Quintal." He stood right up and smiled a big smile.

"I worked with PeeWee Quintal! He was the best man I ever knew". And he went on to describe what I already knew about my uncle. PeeWee was born Edward; the fourth son of a string of five. However, when my husband Bob met him decades later, he astutely noted that he was the "Bull of the Woods".

He was just everybody's hero, animated in his story telling, and supremely magnetic. People just wanted to be near him and associate themselves with him. He was tall and imposing if there was an injustice to be rectified, but light hearted and **enchanting** to those caught in his snare. Nobody ever told a story like uncle Peewee did, except for uncle Black.

One Haloween when I was very young, I saw the dark side of the night. I guess I was in a bit of an experimental stage, and in the fun of the night, we smeared some eggs on Walter Victor's window.

Walter didn't take to it, and came out in his car to find us. He and some of his neighbors were stalking us, and driving rather fast, and he had a flashlight. I was challenged at first, then got spooked as I was chased one way, and my friends another. Separated from the group, I ran off the road and got down in the damp grass right in the middle of the ball field, clinging to the ground, in hopes I was flat enough so as not to be noticeable. That wasn't the best thing to do in retrospect. What lurks in the cool night air, when you're a young kid alone and scared is slightly reminiscent of "something wicked this way comes".

The longer I lay there, the more petrified I became. Stiff and cold. And all the sounds around me I was imagining to be a lynching mob of angered townspeople coming for me. I wanted my mom and dad!

It was starting to feel like pure agony, and I was too scared to get up. Finally, at the zenith of my fear, I heard a motor approaching. It clugged slowly till it stopped, and I could feel the headlights shining on me. I was fully exposed, yet kept my head down, still as a mouse. I heard footsteps, then silence. Time was in slow motion. The form that stood over me was threateningly quiet, and I was waiting for a burst of something..

"Sharon.. is that you" I smiled big, looking up at my dear uncle Peewee; standing there larger than life in the headlights of his pick up truck against the darkness beyond. I bounced up and happily jumped into his cozy truck. He brought me straight home to the store, and within the warm glow of the group gathered there, I recounted my adventure bravely to a laughing response. Such was the reassurance always available from my treasured family . I looked up admiringly at my wonderful, handsome, brave and noble uncle Peewee. He was my very own.

And so. .After hearing Swamiji's voice for all these years, I was wishing that I could have known Master this intimately as well. "Well, why didn't you ask?" He then made himself available through a series of talks SRF had for sale off their web site. Why didn't I think of this before? Having contentedly absorbed his wonderful presence through these CD's, it very early dawned on me; Toto..   I don't think we're in Kansas anymore.

Masters wasn't some lofty personality so culturally and intellectually different from me. There was that slight frenchness in the dialog , the same mannerisms.. There were the same vocal inflections and tonal quality, that delightful expressiveness and love. There was even that irresistable off-shot belly laugh.

He's .. just like my uncle PeeWee.

THAT THOU MIGHTST SEEK IT IN MY ARMS

The place that I think of most as home in this world was the store, where I spent from age 4 till 13, in the little Northern Alberta farming community hamlet called Calahoo, amidst a large nest of family. Dad and mom both ran the business and it was an old style trading store with a big, wide open friendly wooded interior and a broad, rounded tar paper/ brick façade front. There were dry goods, fresh foods, clothes, toys, a cold room and butcher area, a tack room with cowsalt, harnesses, seed etc, and candy. So many happy hours were spent in there comingling with family, neighbors, and the Indians from the reserve. Many many stories were told there, great and valiant stories. And, funny, funny stories. It was the central place of the community, and it held for all of us a most cherished atmosphere. At first there was no running water, and mom got buckets of water from Mrs. Latendre's pump well across the road. We had an outhouse, and it was customary for the Berube boys to sneak into our yard and push it over as a prank on Halloween night. One year, dad had laughingly winched it and pulled it over about 4 feet off of its hole. Imagine the laughter amidst cussing when the boys went to push it over and instead ..Well, we had a 5 gallon pail under a toilet seat in the bathroom in the years that followed. Mom called it our chemical toilet. We all 4 kids took turns bathing in a big tin washtub filled with rainwater from a barrel, heated on the stove. I remember a big smoky kitchen where everybody made a habit of coming to buy something early so mom would invite them in and serve everybody coffee.

All of the enchantments of nature I speak of were initiated the mornings I stepped out of the door of that store, past old Blackie, and out into a world that was my very own treasure. I truly belonged there. Well, after 1970, we left. But, it so happens, in a twist of fate, I was again in Calahoo years later. The store had been un inhabited for many years, and In the mid 90's when my kids were babies, I returned to Calahoo for a short time. It was a time I just, needed.. to go home.

And I was there the very day that great broad faced smiling building was bulldozed down. I happened to be going by in my car with my babies. I saw Grant Berube; a man I had babysat as a youngster, whose dad had pulled Halloween pranks, and along with his many brothers, rivaled the Quintal boys, excelling in sports and gallantries of all kinds. Here Grant was this day, seated in a cat headed towards my beloved childhood home. The now abandoned giant was so dilapidated, but still trying to hold strong and look proud. Indeed, it did look like it had a face, so frantically alarmed but relieved to see me there. And It finally let go..almost bitter-sweetly beconing me..

Slowly it leaned over, saying gooood-bye…..gooood……….bye..

Frank Kolesar, whose family had lived across the road from it for over 40 years, came running over to take pictures. Grant had a sorry look on his face, and couldn't even look at me. He put his head down, and just pushed her over. I will never forget you, I thought. I was inconsolable.

Three thousand miles I had come.

Oh Dearest Master, as I float into your realms of contentment in my meditation, I feel lighter and lighter, until inside the top of my head I feel so free as to soar skyward into your grace. Likened to this was the childhood home you provided me, the existence of which you even guarded through the eyes of a loyal old dog. He too was there at your design, presiding over my house of enchantment from the porch. Those walls also, served as a cranium for my contentment, out of which I could lift upward un hindered, expressing myself as if right out the windows and through the roof to the starry top of all existence. Past the railroad tracks, the elevator, the slough, alfalfa fields, and hills of Calahoo, I could happily wonder from my firm roots below.

Thank you for the home that provided our family with a good life blessed by you. There was always fresh food on the table, and not only that, but room for one more.

I was ennobled to dream the dreams of little girls there within those embracing walls, and not be concerned with the wild winds when the sky was dark.

Dearest home of mine, you took us in when I was not yet far misplaced from the bosom of my Heavenly Father, and could still feel his love vibrating within you. As Mary, I was. Not Margaret, who toiled and fretted over the dinner and the decore. I was free to be the child within my loving environment, to remember my Master, and sit every moment, carefree at the feet of my beloved, washing them with tears of joy and silken hair adorning.

Becoming ever more your child again, Beloved Lord, I do see the need to finally let everything fall away but you.

Perhaps witnessing the destruction of my most beloved earthly home, and at a time when I so desired that manifestation, was your way of pulling me a little closer yet, to your bosom once again.

(devotee)

Were not my pains after all

Shade of thine outstretched hand

Caressing me

(the Lord)

All these things I didst take

Not for thy harms

But that thou mightst seek it

In my arms.

(The Hounds of Hell)

While at Ananda the first time, I attended a kirtan where the devotees from India were leading the chanting. I thought I would only stay for a little while, as I wanted to have a long evening meditation, and get up early to meditate. I was thinking of the times when, as a musician, I would sit through ad lib solo sessions of songs our band would be playing. The soloist would go off into a rapture playing very expansively. I always envied them that, because when I got out into unchartered territory on my guitar, I tended to end up in a train wreck, hitting bad notes or not intuitively feeling a good melodic direction to go in. If I hadn't been nervous about it, I would have felt the path open up I'm sure. But, I was afraid I wouldn't impress people. I always ended up then, playing the way I knew best; the chords that held the rhythm solidly under them. Well, I was getting a little bored when the chants were being repeated over and over. It was reminding me how I used to have to repeat my rhythm guitar parts over and over while someone else got to do the enjoyable part. Then, I became angry with myself. "You are wanting to go back and meditate-- for what? To become free and spontaneous with God. But, you can't even do that here. If you want to feel the divine flowing through you, you have to open to it, let it come in. "

I tried to relax and started lightly clapping my hands and swaying back and forth with the music. I started to see how little nuances of the song were becoming more and more sweet with every rotation of the verses. I started to place new vocal inflections of my own into the verses, building on especially endearing lyrics in expressive new ways. Finally, near the end of the night, at the end of a particularly pretty chant, I opened my eyes and looked around. Everything was bright and lovely. I felt myself inside a warm hum. As I studied everyone sitting around me, I thought; "I didn't know you were here..I never saw you. You either. " The thought occurred to me. "Oh, how I love all of you". Then I looked at the fellow sitting right next to me. He was an Indian guy. As I shyly studied his face, I thought "how beautiful you are. I love You!" We ended the night with the fading melody of Aum, aum, ...(slowly at last) a—u—m. By then my eyes were filled with tears because each of those words sounded just like   H-O-M-E.

THE LEGEND OF GERALD

When I was a child, we used to go on Sunday drives to the houses of old people who lived alone. Perhaps my mom and dad had a softness in their hearts for old folks, and wanted to relieve their loneliness. But, I have a sneaking suspicion they envied them their sanctity and drew from them something intangible, something very beautiful, that my parents themselves deeply needed. For, those we visited indeed, didn't seem lonely at all. In fact, I feel like I crossed the threshold of sacred ground on more than one occasion. The countryside was dotted with the humble abodes of old people who lived alone. Sometimes there was naught but a grassy pathway that led to their places nestled off in the woods. When we as kids went inside, it was enough to sit gazing at the sunlight filtering in through a dusty window, and listen to our parents talk to an old timer. We basked in the sweetness of old fabrics, musty smells, weathered wood, coal oil lanterns, and creaking doors. A love hung thick in the air there. Some kind of indwelling busyness of spirit; a soft murmuring bubbling inside the very walls, waiting for the stillness to return so it could release some glorious secret plan into the day. Sometimes the old barnyards outside too, would enthrall me as to fairly scoop me up into a drifting lullaby and carry me and my imagination off to dreamily play. Later on in life when I thought of yogi's meditating, these scenes came back to me. How blissfully perfect. One could find God in the quiet of a cabin in the countryside veritably hidden in the prairies of Northern Alberta, and no one would ever know, cause you were just **old**. Your Beloved could come and go as He pleased, and you would always have the table set for His visit, with no interruptions. No wonder Master was lingering around here in those days, I thought happily.

Behind the store, our lane extended past a slue, an old building that used to be part of a train station at the tracks, and then dog legged right up a path that led to a white-wall thatched log house that was built by my own Grandpa Quintal when my mom's family was young. Now there were 2 elderly Indian men living there; the Berlau brothers, who used to live in a shack down ol Dick's road on the river at the back of Granny's farm. At least here they had a real house, one that had been grand in its time with an enterprising dad, a mom who kept coyotes for pets and fed a boisterous house full of growing kids. The house had become still and ominous looking, sitting up on the hill alone as it did. The sheds and coops that once housed old timey farming machinery and tools for fixing them, were now containers that echoed the various whistling directions of the breezes, with doors that creaked in an eerie harmony with those drifting melodies. The chickens and cows were no longer strutting and ambling along the many trails, and they were reduced to a thin line of trodden grass made by one young Cree Indian boy. His name was Gerald.

 Nobody ever saw this boy. His mother, after giving birth to him, dropped him off for her two uncles to raise. She also dropped off his older brother Tonto, who acclimated into society quite well, running with the Quintal boys, and not spending much time at the hill-house. Gerald however, was of a different breed. When outside, he hid so as never to be seen, and took to the woods. He spent much of his time inside. What he did in there, I never knew. What was there to do within 4 walls in the 50's? They tried to get him to go to school. He hid in the bushes until the bus was gone. He was so traumatized at the thought of leaving the place, that they never continued trying to make him go. The place just seemed like a small ghost town way up there, and Gerald became like a ghost. And, ghosts are very exciting subjects for playing kids to contemplate.

 There was a Belgian family who had taken over the old Krupa farm just the other side of the tracks, and I played with one of the 2 little boys; Andy Van Imshoot. His mom had a happy round face and wore a babushka on her head. His dad Paul was a handsome artistic man who exuded warmth and humility. His artwork was so fine that the wooden Stations of the Cross in the Calahoo church were his hand made intricately carved scenes of the journey of Jesus. Andy was a white headed boy with the lightest blue eyes, and didn't speak any English for the first few months of our friendship.

As we got to be bosom buddies, however, we got better and better at understanding each other. Playing near the tracks, as close as we did to the hill-house, we found ourselves being lured closer and closer by the legend of Gerald. Then came the day we saw him.

 That first day I don't believe we spoke, him or us. Gerald was like a wild animal that finally after a time of still curiosity from a distance, began to relax enough that we were able to draw closer, as if looking through the underbrush for something interesting. I had a baseball cap on and I think he thought I was a boy. The second day we went back, and he seemed a bit excited. We walked the trails and he showed us one of the sheds that had a table and a rocking chair in it. This was his playhouse! How wonderful. I remember his voice being deep. He only said 2 or three words at a time. He must have been 11 or 12, and we were maybe 6 and 7. He had an aura of a different time and place about him; a stillness that was a very stark contrast to my fidgeting. He calmed me. I liked it.

We grew to like being with Gerald. However, nature being what it is, Gerald started to glean a bit of the outside world from us. One day we were at the old train station, and Gerald began whispering things in Andy's ear, then they'd both look over at me and giggle. I didn't have my baseball cap on. It occurred to me that Gerald had started perceiving me as a little girl. Suddenly it seemed like it was them versus me..I was different. I'll never forget later in Gerald's dark cob webby playhouse how he came to me while I was rocking in the old rocking chair. He put both his hands on the arms of the chair, stopping the motion and looked down long at me, right into my eyes. I felt vulnerable, perhaps in a way I never had before. Playing again at the train yard, when they began to behave towards me in a giggling fashion again, I shot out in a fit of rage at Andy, beat him up, and stomped off home. Gerald did nothing but watch in wonderment.

I never went back there. I started to drift into other areas of interest in my play. By the time Gerald was 17, after being a recluse all those years, we heard he was rushed to the hospital. He had not been exposed to any childhood diseases and his body hadn't developed much immunity. Somehow he contracted scarlet fever.

The Berlau boys didn't even have a car or a phone, so it was pretty late before they solicited help. Gerald died. Probably partly from the shock of even being in a hospital. I felt so sorry for him, and was very reflective about the life He had lived. I thought it was a horrible life, but now it seems to me to have been a privileged one. To be able to come to terms with yourself that way, having no distractions,could have been an advancement if one was spiritually inclined. I wonder if Gerald had some karma to work out, that only required him to be a hermit of sorts for a time. It's not that easy to get born into a family that's not enmeshed in the world. The Berlau boys were simple men, illiterate and quite base. Gerald, though, was something deeper, I thought. Whatever lay deep in that primitive spirit of his, may have been something on a level of bliss I had no access to.

These kinds of spirits were scattered amongst the crude living quarters of the Indians on the wide open Alexander Reservation too. I knew that intuitively. Some of them did work outside the Reserve, or farm land within it. Many however, used the community property built by the government for them, simply as kind of props that were in the way of their natural habitat. The houses got run down, and they never did make much use of furniture. But, the ones that didn't turn to alcohol were somehow regal and free, able to yet be the people of their Gods.
When I would ride my motorbike through there on the way to Sandy lake,
I would sometimes see some special one peering at me, in a noble kind of way, like a cougar who had been startled by an intruding pioneer in the deep forest.

These are the times I would think of Gerald. Tansi Neestow ;
Godspeed my brother

There's a redman on a hill   looking out over the plain
he takes aim and lets an arrow fly
tonight there'll be a ceremony for the hunter and the kill
he gives thanks to the abalone sky

(chorus)
Indian eyes gaze out across the nation
Indian eyes smile on the setting sun
deep in the night they will find the lighted darkness
Indian Eyes

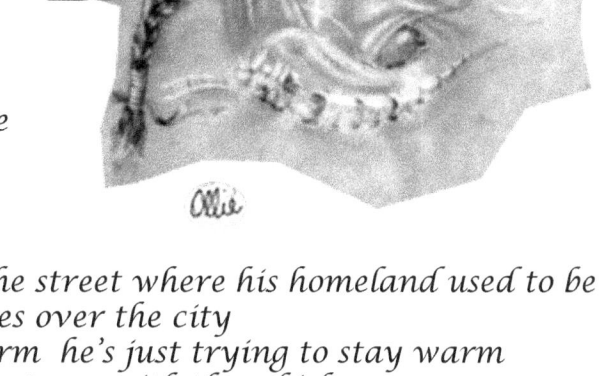

Well the whiteman
crossed the water
with a bible and a gun
and the warrior
heard a warning
from the raven

but the spirit
wasn't broken
for the few that
had survived
were waiting when
the smoke began to rise

(chorus)

There's a redman on the street where his homeland used to be
and a grey cloud passes over the city
he won't cause any harm   he's just trying to stay warm
and he's riding out the storm with the whiskey

he's got nowhere to go   he don't know where to turn
and he feels a fire burning deep within him
he lays down in a doorway drifts off into the night
suddenly the eagle takes to flight

(chorus)

(song by Allen Estes, Tom Grant and Sharon; the group "Trinity Lane")

I notice in Ollie's drawings, her faces are so familiar. The indian chief indeed does look very much like our uncle Chief. He was the oldest Quintal brother; serenely percolating inside with a substance so potent, but that he kept at bay so as to fit into the everyday realm of our simple prairie life. He didn't dwell on wealth. He worked and kept beautiful horses, weaving intricate leather saddlery and tack implements with many colored patterns and braids.

He would look at us with a threatening deadly stare sometimes, and raise his voice to a thunder. And then --once we were sufficiently scared, we could suddenly no longer detect a trace of care in his countenance. And poker faced, he'd crack a joke. Uncle Chief thought to take me across the border on a dusty day in his pick up, to the social security office near Omak Washington to initiate my United Native Nations status. This very act would facilitate my allowance to work years later, in the United States of America. It would declare to my timid nature, that there is no border for the free in spirit. Chief made it so. He lay in the hospital not many years later, with cancer. At 4 in the morning I sat up in bed and looked at the clock. I had been travelling a trail through the basin of the reservation between Oliver and Osoyoos and in my dream, had turned to see on those grassy plains, a grand ceremony lit by the very opening of the sky, and my uncle's spirit lifting to the rhythmic majesty of sound and dance orchestrated by a vast band of Indians. They were united as one in this profound offering gesture.
I learned later, that that morning at 4, uncle was heard by his attending nurse to whisper a quiet "good-bye"..

I've been considering why I feel more anxiety in life while I'm trying to perfect my meditation techniques. It seems to me that when I was projecting my life outwardly at every turn, I was fairly content at a base level of existence. Once I started enlisting conscious efforts to redirect thoughts and feelings inward toward the spine, I started developing a feeling of discomfort. It would be easier at that point to let go and assume old habits, I thought. But, It's natural to go through this if you think about it. Remember when you learned how to swim properly; you made a constant effort to stop the 'frog kick' action in your swim stroke. Instead of pumping them you wanted to learn to straighten the legs and paddle them uniformly. This felt very awkward, and you actually sunk until you started to gain momentum enough in your practice to be buoyant. After you began to swim properly though, you soared through the water effortlessly, not like a frog, but a fish.

COMANCHE

When I come home from my desk job, on most weekdays, I take a little exercise by riding my bike 4 times up Akins Ridge road. I kind of reign victorious over this practice because, instead of straining and plodding up that slope, I am forever in my heart, simply topping Snooky's hill in the gravel, amidst wide open wheat fields, on my way to Granny's farm to play.

One rather aimless summer day in the early 60's, Vickie and I decided to go riding horses. We were at the Diamond Willow Ranch of our uncle PeeWee; father of our cousin Granny (as in Granny Goodwitch from the Sugarcrisp-Sugarbear cereal commercials. She had always worn the little round wire framed glasses, thus got the name). I was staying over at Vickies, and she lived in a trailer in the yard at the farm. Her dad was uncle Shmoe. Granny was a couple years younger than us, and a regular Annie Oakley. She was literally raised with the livestock. She took to it from a toddler age when already she would ride a miniature Shetland pony like a barrel racer. I remember the story that she turned up missing one day, and aunty found her in between Gornter the sow's suckling piglets in the muddy corral. Granny ruled the ranch. She was the instigator of all that was fun, whether it was riding the horses full tilt across the fields or through the pond, exploring the woodland trails throughout the back acres, remodeling the treehouses, building tunnels of bails in the hay shed, or perfecting some 'way up high' jump into the straw. She was just a master at finding fun things to do, and we all naturally fell in behind her. You had to be tough though; she was hard to keep up with and extremely demanding. Around the horses, there was no nonsense. Even the horses knew to behave.

Well, this particular day, Granny wasn't with us. We decided to go behind the little red barn into the large corralled area that backed the river, and catch Comanche and Apache to take a ride.

Comanche was a big quarter Welch cross, and Apache, as far as I can remember was a smaller quarter –pinto cross. But Comanche was wily. I liked riding him, however I was always a bit wary after I saw him one time pull a trick on Big Red (my cousin and Granny's older sister). We were all bolting away in a line from the farm in the first field toward Calahoo, and Comanche doubled back lickety split and headed back toward the barn. He left Red still headed the other direction. Such was the finesse of the switch, that she actually continued in the air before hitting the dirt. Well, I wanted to ride him. His trot was such a comfortable lope, and his gallop so rhythmic. Vickie and I looked at the two horses. Comanche looked over and smirked "you kids..where's Granny..no Granny? Well, I'm not sure I feel like going out today.." He ambled out towards the river, Apache following him. We had oats, but he was smart. He said No. Well, we followed them to the back corner by the river, and having them cornered, tried to bridle them with a rope. But they just kicked up a little fuss and got through us.

We spent the morning and the better part of the afternoon following them around trying to corner them. Finally just for fun Comanche stopped and let us get him. We led them back into the barn to get the good bridles on. We were a bit shaken, and nervous after this test of wills. Comanche was calm as a cucumber. I was holding the bottom half of the back barn door when he came up to it, looked at me, looked out at the bush, looked back at little me again, and proceeded to push his chest against the bottom half of the barn door. "Vickie!" I cried. She came running and we both pushed on the door with all our mights. Comanche just walked through, and trotted out into the woods. We let Apache go, and headed back to the house.

When I listen to Swamiji's beautiful music, much of it tends to take me back to various journeys through Granny's farm. "Love is the dawn of Understanding" is one such beautiful song. Or, " Land of Mystery".

And even that day with its weariness, I do remember that portion of the farm up against the river, our beloved river, and those woods where I still can see how the morning sun was filtering in through the trees as we followed our horses..how morning happily shifted to noon and beyond, with the warming and busyness of nature swelling, bursting, and becoming quiet again.

Even that trying day there were thoughts in my head of the refreshing stillness of a morning walk a young Indian girl might have taken through these paths on her way to gather some water hundreds of years ago. The high trace of a hawk overhead was always just pure blessedness to see. And, if you ever got to hear the lonesome cry of a loon, that is something you would never ever forget, for sure.

... any end to evolution?" a visitor once asked Paramhansa Yogananda. "No end," the Master replied. "Progress goes on until you achieve **endlessness**.".

Dear God, as I hustle and bustle and paint myself into corners these days, thank you for letting me know, that the journey is important. There is no final destiny.

AND IN THE SWEETNESS OF FRIENDSHIP

LET THERE BE LAUGHTER AND SHARING OF PLEASURES

FOR   IN THE DEW OF LITTLE THINGS

THE HEART FINDS IT'S MORNING

AND IS REFRESHED   (Kahlil Gibran)

There's a certain way you can crack a baseball with a bat, or follow through on a golf swing, even smack a volleyball on a spike, that makes it sizzle. And, you didn't use a lot of force. It was finesse. You allowed a flow of spiritual power into your medulla to assist you in a most glorious way. That is how I'm starting to finally feel with my energization exercises. I squeeze my muscle, and hear that little gong ring hit the top at the fair when you lifted your mallet and hit the pad with your best shot.

Girls' Volleyball

Top row: Coach-Mrs. Clayton. Marianne Wahl, Jane Collingwood, Iris Mackenzie, Antonie Clarke
Sitting: Sue Yamamoto, Sharon Anderson, Gloria Simpson, Pat Ponich, Kathy Kannigan, Nancy Binet.

HOW GREEN IS MY VALLEY

Having tried for years to come to terms with the glaring flaws I was finding in myself, I began also to sorrow at the disappearance of my innocent childhood perceptions. Flaws started to appear everywhere in my life in slow succession, morphing and becoming grotesque at times. My parent's strength started to seem like a cover, and deep divides started to show. My mom hid things from my dad so he wouldn't get angry. He felt increasingly unvalued and disengaged. He held it against her. She would start to take medication for the knots in her stomach. As a child she had been temporarily given to her grandmother to raise during an illness to her mother, and was instead left there for the remainder of her childhood to be treated as a farm worker. She would not know the happiness the rest of the Quintal kids knew. She only knew unwavering loyalty to a mean old woman, and deep, hidden envy. She had given me enormous freedoms in life, as an attempt to vicariously recapture some freedom herself. Life then became a tragedy for her as she slowly realized nothing would improve. I loved her more than anything but knew I was losing her. As I entered my teens we had moved to the beautiful fruit belt; the Okanagan valley nestled in the Rocky Mountains near the southern British Columbia border. At first I thrived making friends in our little town of Winfield. I excelled in almost all sports you could think of trying, and even made the first string of the volleyball team that would give me the experience of placing third in the provincials.

I think many of my spiritual disciplines were gained from my devotion to honing my abilities in these arenas. There was a great power to be harnessed in learning to hang 3 feet up in the air at the net and slam a ball down hard with just the right crack, aiming just where there was nobody placed on the other side to retrieve it. The cheers were intoxicating. Or, not letting your team mates down by diving pointedly under a spike from your back row, to shoot a lost ball up again and back into play. Blocking effectively was exciting too. Perhaps the best practice was perfecting a sizzling spiked serve, 21 times in a row without missing.

This was rarely done and was akin to pitching a no hitter. I don't recall if I ever succeeded in perfectly serving a game, but I could do it in practice to be sure. It served as an opportunity for a subtle study. Performing my kriya breaths, years later in meditating, I would summon a similar kind of stamina for consistency.

The little town of Winfield was like a garden paradise of fruit orchards and crystal clear lakes, in the heart of a friendly little mountain valley that displayed lush, almost tropical trees amongst which I loved the giant weeping willows and majestic ponderosa pines. In those days it was a still rustic place with simple family businesses, pretty winding roads, and long summer days were spent there on the happy beaches diving off cliffs and the packing plant roof. I wish I had known about kriya then, and that stamina could help you a great deal to reach God. I had it. My friend had a farm at the bottom of the Crown land (Belonging to the Queen of England) we called Wrinkle Face mountain. There was no development on that face thus, and it was a paradise for horse-back riding. The sunny slopes were enchanted up there, and you could taste the stillness of that wide open range with a panoramic view of the valley beyond. I was in the first stages of a rather distressing change of direction down there in that valley below, with an incessant urge building in me to find upheavals in my life, and parties to lose myself in. Up here though, I was the little girl from Calahoo very capably riding my horse.

I grew to love an Arab horse named Alabar. When we started out with the bunch of us, he would always spark a race, and then take off on me. I would become indignant and think competitively "If you wana run, By God, you're gona run!", and I would kick into each stride, not allowing him to let up, and finally we would find ourselves miles ahead of the rest, stopping at HorsePee pond for a break. It fell so quiet there as he settled into grazing and I lay back in some tall grass under a tree. All we could hear was each other's panting, and the buzzing of a horsefly here and there. We made up then, glancing at each other admiringly, and felt such a nice magnetism; me and Alabar. I was lucky to have somewhat mastered him. I saw him scrape Larry Carruthers off his back on a dead run, under a wire that was stretched across an old fence line.

I felt like I could have lived on that mountain. Perhaps I could have made a hovel in one of the old mining caves farther up. Farther up still was the solitude, remote Beaver lake area, where I had caught a garbage bag full of rainbow trout off the bank with a bobber, on an endless summer day with my friend Jerry. Then we had proudly brought them home down that curving gravelly road on my motorbike. What was it in me that was making me so restless. There was a knawing in my stomach most of the time. I wanted more but didn't know what I wanted. I loved it here on the mountain..but I would have to go back down.

   I felt a need to go to grade 12 in the bigger town of Kelowna. I had the most wonderful friends in Winfield. It was the most nurturing wholesome environment, but something in me wanted more action. At this bigger more impersonal school, I sought to be accepted amongst a group that were not very good mentors for me. I dove into a sort of lazy existence that depended on sense stimulations to inspire or rouse me to any active level of feelings. I lost interest in my school work, and got into trouble. I guess I was trying to escape life in a way.

One lazy summer, I had a chance to detach myself from my problems altogether for a morning, and see life a whole different way. Part of the reason our Okanagan valley seemed so serene was not only that some of the land was Crown land, but also that a great deal of it had been deemed to the United Native Nations, in reparation for them losing so much of it in earlier times. My dad built a big mobile home park on this land with a special permit. And, we lived next to the base of Beaver Lake road that winded up our side of old Wrinkle Face. Between us and the end of the tree line, lived several families of Indians. They were literally in no man's land..and were nomads in the current sense of the word. They had no work to do, and didn't particularly take to the buildings that had been built for them. They became little rundown shacks alongside grassy clearings and brush piles. My friend Richard and I one morning had been riding little mini motorcycles out behind the trailer park on the big dirt piles, and we came across a curious, almost surreal setting. We quietly hid behind a mound of grass, and settled down for an hour or more watching this scene.

Around a brush pile were about 8 Indian people. There were some liquor bottles strewn, and a few cups. They were sleeping hap hazardly here and there, in any old position on the ground or across logs, looking very comfortable. One by one, they would slowly awaken. I felt like I was watching a den of lions in Africa. They just turned any direction and wondered off that way. Not one of them said a word to any of the others. They just rather, leaned into the breeze and lit off softly and happily. I felt sorry, and contented all at the same time. How I wished in the deep recesses within me, that I was unattached like this. How I marveled at the freedom.

Well, I did have to somehow fit into the framework of things, and my problems hadn't gone anywhere. However, I did find stability and solace in my music. I always had that. Since an early age my mom had urged me to play songs at family get-togethers. Now I found a group of older fellows; family men, who needed a front singer for their band. They liked me, and we started playing weekend bookings around the valley. This gave me something constructive to do, and from then on I was always working on some music project. I was a folkie too in those days. I loved James Taylor, Joni Mitchell, and Cat Stevens. That kind of music to this day brings me back to those rolling orchards, and wide grassy grins of those rambling mountains. The melodies seep down through deep pools of clear aqua blue lake water into the bubbling essence of my untouched soul. I wasn't to stay in my valley though.

There were other plans in the ether.

Nobody can teach you anything.
We have to recognize reality.
All truth, all spiritual experience, all divine awakening
takes place by memory.
We remember who we are. You see it and say "But of course!"
This remembering is the whole process of the spiritual path.
I came upon the Bhagavad Gita, and I read that.
And I found myself so thrilled with this scripture,
that talked in terms of an expansion of consciousness;
talked of the need to justify your beliefs by actual experience,
talked in terms of God as something so vast as not to be limited
by a particular form or religion or one particular creed.

Swamiji

I was fishing at a lovely spot on a river in a thickly wooded area, with 2 friends; Jack and Roger. I was 16. It was a warm day, and I had on a two piece bathing suit, getting a little sun there on the bank. When I had to go to the bathroom, I just walked out into the bushes.

But, I squatted on a wasps nest. At first I heard the buzzing sound. The next thing I knew I was in a frenzy of angry wasps. Was this payback time? I bolted into a dead run through underbrush where there was not even a faint trail. Over and over again I was being stung as I ran, and I became numb with fear. The branches were cruelly jabbing and cutting my skin, and the blood started to drip from the many cuts. Both pieces of my bathing suit got torn off of me, and I was bare naked. Still, I ran. I ran to out race the fear. I ran to tear off the shame. I ran to be free. I ran and ran. Faster and faster.

I finally came to the clearing about a mile away, where our car was parked. There was no one around, but still I was very traumatized by being naked. I felt exposed from the inside out.

This morning at the spiritual eye, I was squinching to focus there before relaxing, and I used that pressure to aid my running; my trying to break free. Presently I came to a clearing in the forest, where Babaji and his disciples were. I was naked before him. My pride had been scraped off by the many tree branches. My fear had dissipated into the sheer terror that had surrounded me. I stood lowly and calm before him. Now, Babaji, will you let me in? I felt a warmth. Maybe, soon..

Aaron diving off the packing plant roof
Okanagan Center 1975

JUST SING

Near the end of the 70's I was sent back to northern Alberta to live with my aunt and uncle who would have a better rein on me. They lived close to Edmonton and I took my first real job there at AGT; the Alberta Government Phone company. It wasn't long though, before I was singing in the lounges of that city. I enrolled in a music college, and there a curious period in my life ensued.

Of course, I had been singing for a living. But here I had a renowned singing teacher "Dasha Goody" who had a vibrato in her voice. I had a bit of a natural tremelo. She sought to rid me of this feature of my nature, and in the process I began to lose confidence in my ability to sing. On stage I was a natural but here, subject to the judgments of Dasha and the other students in the confines of a study room with only a piano and no familiar guitar, I struggled with the proper diaphragmatic breathing and throat placements of notes she was trying to encourage out of me. It was too sterile. I would often break down and cry. I knew I could do better. Such was the development of another spiritual lesson for my future. I went for months in this low esteemed stupor. Finally I resolved to the fact that maybe I never had been a decent singer after all. Dasha would always leave me out of the rosters to do the feature concert presentations on stage in the performance hall.

One day, she was especially kind, and quietly told me I could sing in a presentation. "Choose a song you have confidence in" she said. I had charts made out for a progressive funky little tune with an infectious ride, and perky little horn lines punctuating it. It was quite aptly called "Don't change horses in the middle of a stream" by the Oakland group Tower of Power. I loved this song and knew it inside and out. My aunty Skinny bought me a velvety long brown dress for the occasion with feathers on the ties. It was beautiful. When my name was announced, I came groovin out on the stage happy as a lark, and proceeded to tear that song up!

I mean, I went for it. I was free to be me now. I guess I kinda forgot everything she was teaching me and went from my gut and my heart. Torbin, Lindsay, Louis and Rob Hughes were premier musicians who all four went on to regional fame in the industry. They were my stage band, and they were rockin.

At the end I was so astonished to see Dasha running toward me with a smile all across her face. She embraced me, almost in tears and uttered, "I..didn't know you could sing".

When you know something I thought, don't ever doubt it. Years later when I hit the low crags deep down into my search for God, I had the tool of this experience under my belt, and was deeply thankful for it. And when in my sadhna, I reach toward realms that I know are there, but they don't reveal themselves, I smile and say to Swamiji.."I will wait".

Fight for your limitations and sure enough they'll be yours.

(Richard Bach: Illusions)

Master's guru; Sri Yukteswar said that enlightenment is like a bird in a cage remembering it is free to fly. At first if you open the door, however, it cowers—afraid of the great opening, not remembering what it was born to do.

One time I had a booking to play in Terrace BC. I was in my early 20's. It was 1000 miles from where I lived in Edmonton, which was already way north in Alberta. I drove and drove. The road became the only sign of civilization in a great forest of wilderness. The rain began to pour heavily, and on the side of the road, I could make out a small form in the mist. It was a young man, with his thumb out. I stopped and let him in dripping wet. He was very quiet, and when he did try to speak , it was French. His long curly hair was matted and the rain compelled off of it rather like it did off his woolen sweater. He smiled gratefully. As we curved our way through the great trees, he awkwardly related to me that he was looking for a job as a lumberjack. I thought he was far too slightly built and too soft spoken to mix with such company. He said he was from a little village not far from Paris, in France. He was so far from home, timid and shaking. Finally, hours later we descended into the town of Terrace, and I made my way to the central Hotel there to sign in. It was still miserably raining. I couldn't leave him on the street on such a dismal note. I instructed him to wait, and after registering, I sneaked him to my room, and we made a pallet for him on the floor. We barely spoke, as the language barrier was extensive. But, after the first few days, we became comfortable with each other's company and soon we could sense the smiles even if they weren't written on the faces. I was singing in the lounge, and the manager didn't seem to like me or my music much. Maybe it was because there weren't too many patrons coming in. Mostly they came to watch the football games on the big tv. He didn't like the fact that he had to pay me when they wanted to watch the game, and I had to sit it out. Sometimes, during my songs, I would look over towards the door to see my beautiful friend peering in with a big smile. He didn't come in. He had no money with which to be frivolous. I made us good sandwiches and we sometimes took walks together during the days. He looked awfully hard for work, but couldn't seem to find a lumber camp that would take him. He was getting a little discouraged. Finally one day, he told me he was going to travel farther up. I walked with him down the hi-way to the outskirts of town. We stood there in silence for a long time, looking down. Then finally, I cheerfully said "Well, good luck Pierre". I gave him a big long hug. Then, I reached in my pocket and handed him a harmonica. "To have music, right in your pocket!" I said, smiling. To my surprise, he reached into his knapsack, and withdrew a book, handing it to me. It was 'Jonathan Livingston Seagull', by Richard Bach. Tears rolled down my cheek as I watched my only friend reduced to a dot over my shoulder, walking back into town. I kept turning to wave. He looked like a little boy. When I got back to my room I opened my new friend to the first page. It was to become my first introduction to the spirit of the bird within the soul of man. And, there, most carefully handwritten; "To the little singer with the big heart"   Love, Pierre.

Sometimes I miss Swamiji so. I listen to him speaking my lessons in the headphones, and see his picture..and a longing aches deep within me. So much so, that I sometimes break down and find myself utterly hopelessly lost in loneliness. These are the times Master comes in short order. And, as Divine mother he loves me tenderly and brings me back. As I erected myself once again in my chair, and gazed at him thankfully, I began listening to a passage from one of his audio CDs. Instantly I heard another voice distinct within Master's voice. Yes, there was Uncle Peewee there, even Uncle Chief in that fatherly gathering presence. But, now there was another. I became still and listened closely. Yes, it was a familiar hearty laugh with a particular sigh. Stretch. The boy who had lived in the store before us, maybe 6 years older than me, and whose mother had been the sister of the woman who is my Aunty Mary; married to Uncle Black. Yes it was Stretch. "Master", I thought.."why has this come so keenly to my attention".. Master looked at me intently. I sat back, and was transported to my last trip home to Calahoo, maybe seven years ago. It hurts me to think of these visits, as I miss my homeland so very much. I was at my sister Ollie's house, walking from the car to the house with the kids, and a big old black pick up truck came barreling down the road, and suddenly screeched to a halt some 20 yards up the road. There appeared a big farmer with a beaming face, running towards me with outstretched arms. He scooped me up and almost swallowed me, vibrating with sentiment. It was Richard Krupa; Stretch. Never had I known him to behave this way. He was reserved and quiet usually. I had been moved to the very depths of my heart, as tears came to both our eyes. Now the tears began to flow even greater as I thankfully nodded to my beautiful Guru. Thank you Master. I surely needed that.

Springtime Johnny

sun was on the hillside
snow was all around
but for the crackling of the campfire
you couldn't hear a sound

then his eyes would twinkle
his chin on his guitar
and in the time it took to sing
my heart was on the wing
and our back door wasn't far

(chorus)
Springtime Johnny
blue Canadian Rockies
I been kinda lonesome
play that song for me
your voice has found a
trail that goes
through the acres of the
sweet grass hills I know
dreams that never fade
happy children played
four strong winds ago

miles fell behind us
years flew out ahead
harsh winds have torn the canyons
leaving grey upon my head

spring had turned to summer
then winter crept in slow
was it just a dream
did i just see a gleam
within the fire's glow

(chorus)

song by sharon

'In the blue Canadian rockies
spring is silent through the trees
and the golden poppies are blooming
round the banks of lake Louise.'

In the mid 80's against a backdrop of staggering beauty that was the skyline near Whistler mountain,

An ol cowboy sang to Bow and I, songs that he wrote ; sweetly reminiscent of 'The Blue Canadian Rockies "
and "Four strong winds"; songs that he had shared amongst the hearty ranch hands of northern Alberta
in the 50's and 60's in the bunkhouses and around the campfires of those mystic prairie lands.

I could see how thoughts like "This is my Sky" could have welled up in the heart of a young Ian Tyson as Johnny's voice and simple guitar strokes trailed off softly into the night.
His was a timeless contribution to what would become a trilogy for the Canadian West;
It's iconic free spirited minstrel Canadian cowboys.

And so it was that in his last years, Johnny had wondered back into the Squamish country,
and befriended a duo of impressionable songsters playing at a café in Whistler.
Johnny was to fall on the ice and break his hip that winter.
He had no money, and I helped him pay his hospital bill.
He was determined in the months that followed, to try and pay me back somehow.
He relentlessly wrote letters to the Tommy Hunter show until at last I was signed up to sing my song Calahoo;
a song I had sneaked in through a back door and dropped onto the desk of Larry Donohue at CFCW radio in Camrose.
Thus was started a career for me. Twenty six years later, Johnny has drifted into my dreams giving me this little song.
Let us lift up our hearts and salute the sons of our rich musical heritage.
Let us not forget the springtime, or Johnny Fulton.

I AM THE ROSE OF SHARON

AND THE LILY OF THE VALLEYS (solomen 2)

I was in Nashville Tennessee. I had worked a whole winter up at Whistler, singing at the ski lodge with Bow, and saving my money. Not to mention skiing every day off that majestic peak. Whether blistering down her front side in ten minutes from top to bottom, joyously swooshing in and out of her bumps, or lofting great leaps through steep sweet powder with the hard core nortic type boys who let me traverse her wild back side with them, I would finally swing down to the lodge just before 3, take off my skis and jump up on the stage. But now, here I was in Nashville. At first I was like a kid in a candy store. I wrote music and met young up and coming song writers and performers like me. Many long held desires manifested as I became more and more creatively confident, and my efforts were being noticed.

I did an album for Curb records, and one for Capitol. But, some darker tendencies were coming out in me. With the possibility of fame and money, they were karmically brought to the surface. Had I known the potential down falls as I do now, perhaps I could have been victorious over them. Alas, I was to learn some deep painful lessons. Now I see it was good. Best to get it over with in this lifetime. I still have time to work on my personality and much more subtly now, having gone through that confusing time. It could have wiped me out completely, and almost did. Then I would have been none the wiser in my next life. So, I am thankful. I had gotten attached to one boyfriend, then another, and when I was miserable the music suffered. The music business had some very questionable characters in it too, and I found myself being paranoid and greedy. My state of mind brought on instability within the publishing and record companies, and I was prone to mood swings. I plunged into a deep depression just before my record deal fell through.

One day I found myself in a laundry mat waiting for my clothes to dry, and I was utterly lost. I was homesick and heartsick over having lost the child in me that had known such happiness. The person I saw in my reflection on the dryer window now was alien to me in so many ways.

I looked for a magazine on the bookshelf there, and there was only a bible. Here I was in the bible belt of the Southern United States. Surely, I thought, there must be some kind of answer in there. I picked it up, and with tears rolling down my cheeks I asked "God.. what do you want me to know?.." Then I opened it randomly somewhere in the middle and my eyes fell on my own name;

I am the Rose of Sharon and the Lily of the Valleys. (solomen)

I pitilessly broke down and pleaded with God. "Take my life. I don't know where to turn. Oh my dearest Lord, please help me" I cried..

WHY IS THE WORLD SO CRUEL   WHY AM I SUCH A FOOL
BELIEVING I WAS AN EXCEPTION TO THE RULE
WHY DOES A KITTEN DIE   ON A COLD WINTER DAY ON THE HIWAY
WHY DO I ALWAYS CRY---
WHY AM I ALL ALONE JUST WHEN I NEED SOMEONE
WHERE CAN I GO   I CAN'T THINK OF ONE PLACE I KNOW
I FEEL LIKE I'M FADING AWAY   WILL THERE EVER COME A DAY
I FIND MY WAY BACK HOME---
SEEMS I WAS BORN TO BE   A DRIFTER ON A STORMY SEA
SENDING MY S-O-S   INTO THE WIND
CAN ANYBODY HEAR ME   DOES ANYBODY KNOW WHERE I'M HEADED FOR
WHICH WAY DO I TURN   TO GET BACK TO THE SHORE---
THEN CAME A LIFELINE   FROM THE DEPTHS OF THIS HEART OF MINE
I LET GO   AND YOUR SPIRIT GRIPPED MY SOUL
AND I TURNED AND FACED THE SUN   AND I SAID THY WILL BE DONE
AND I TURNED THIS LIFE AROUND---
CAUSE I WASN'T BORN TO BE A DRIFTER ON A STORMY SEA
SENDING MY S-O-S   INTO THE WIND
FINALLY I WAS READY   FINALLY I KNEW WHERE I WAS HEADED FOR
AND I ANSWERED THAT QUIET KNOCK   UPON MY DOOR   (song by Sharon)

THE MANY CHAPTERS
OF BOBBY CROWELL

EVERY NOW AND THEN THE THINGS I LEAN ON LOSE THEIR MEANING

AND I FIND MYSELF CAREENING

IN PLACES WHERE I SHOULD NOT LET ME GO

HE HAS THE POWER TO GO WHERE NO ONE ELSE CAN FIND ME

YES AND TO SILENTLY REMIND ME

OF THE HAPPINESS AND GOOD TIMES THAT I KNOW

....

I FEEL FINE ANYTIME HE'S AROUND ME

AND HE'S AROUND ME NOW   ALMOST ALL THE TIME

IF I'M WELL YOU CAN TELL   THAT HE'S BEEN WITH ME

HE'S BEEN WITH ME NOW   QUITE A LONG LONG TIME

YES AND I FEEL FINE   (James Taylor)

To find joy in life's moments.
Where to begin..
The older I got, the more I was feeling like a prisoner
in my own skin;
claustrophobic as if needing to get out of a dark closet.
But, my meditation has helped me to strengthen my heart.
I practice gripping with it; reaching out to Guru with intense love.
And so it is that instead of being driven to try and flee from pain,
I am beginning to perceive the beautiful mellow light of intuition.
A sign that something else works better;
The longing to do for another.
And, when a moment begins to torture me,
projecting me outward in turmoil,
and alienating my spirit from this body it dwells in,
I am beginning to feel for this moment too.
Poor moment, filled with anxiety.
You need love. You need to belong.
You are my moment. Let my heart grip you.
Come to me, stay and be content here within.
When you have passed,
I will set you free to fly away
and disappear.

MY HELP COMETH

Around the time I was being born in 1955 in Northern Alberta, there was, down South in Tennessee, a little boy of 8 living in the projects with his ma and his two brothers. His older sisters **and brother** were already married and his pop was off hoboing around Jimmy Rogers style somewhere. The boy's name was Bobby and he'd been born of a humble redheaded Irish girl in a train stop holler called Tidwell Switch. After that they lived in a series of places where you could see through the boards and floors. When they moved, it was usually because it was rent time, and they pretty much filled the same wagon with all they had and pulled it off down the road. When they got to live in the projects (or slum housing), that was 'high cotton' for them. It was the only time they ever had heat and water, and a solid roof over their heads. But most of the time, they couldn't get in to live there.

Sometimes they didn't eat for days on end. Bobby learned at a young age how to be industrious. He'd get a paper route, caddy at the golf course, pitch in helping anyone with anything, or even steal off of a grocery truck to bring something home for them to eat. One time he got a whole case of wieners and treated all the kids in the neighborhood to a wiener roast around a big bon fire. He'd stop by the donut shop and ask for the cripples (the ones that were shaped wrong) or the holes. People got used to him stopping by on his route, and liked his happy-go-lucky attitude. He'd ask if he could sweep floors, or wash windshields at the gas station. Whenever he could, he'd wiggle in to see how a car was being fixed, and before he was old enough to drive, he had put a car together from parts, and rebuilt a transmission. He was a most amazing child, looking back on his life.

He was to be my husband. This desperate situation I found myself in down here in the Bible Belt beckoned his destined entrance into my world.

I thought I had come to Nashville for the music, which was in itself a momentous life lesson to learn. But no. It was much more than that. My meeting this man was a life altering blessing and a welcome about-face in my directionless life. I grew in the 20 years that have passed since I met Bobby, to realize that I would never have become refined in spirit enough to even follow Master's teachings had God not guided me this 3000 some odd miles away, into the back yard of Bobby Crowell. It is indeed an honor in these pages to tell of his childhood and life, as he would never presume to do such a thing for himself. This remarkable story will at least be told somewhat here for me to introspect upon and marvel at, if nobody else ever reads this.

He was very intelligent, but they could never stay in the same school long enough to make progress. Someone would make fun of their tattered clothes, and he'd throw down right then and there. He got used to fighting, and got very accomplished at it. It saddened me too, to hear how some of the teachers treated the kids from the projects. At one point, he was eligible for free lunch tickets, but the teacher would bleat out loudly from the front of the room, in front of everybody "All the kids who need tickets, come up and get them!" Bob opted out. Even if someone offered him a plate, he'd say "No thanks, I'm not hungry". But his belly was always hurting. He used to play hooky and go, of all places, to the *library*. There he would drink in history, science, geography, and philosophy like a rare nectar. He couldn't believe it was free to have this privilege, and he would read encyclopedias by the volumes in his spare time. He also became familiar with the great classic writers of America. He loved Steinbeck and Mark Twain. He could also quote Shakespear and the Bible from a young age.

Bobby used to stay sometimes with his paternal grandmother; a stern disciplinarian who lived modestly way back in the country.

He remembers her being an imposing force. So much so, that she was able to levitate a table right off the floor with her concentration. He didn't know what to think about that, and put it on a shelf in his mind, so to speak.

But he was never able to dispute the fact that this thing happened. My childhood held a lot of fanciful notions, but as far as I know, nothing like this ever happened out our way. It wasn't until I met Bob in the old South, did I actually hear of such things really happening to somebody.

One time he said he went to a Pentecostal tent meeting. He used to go to these events and church, because often they would give out a biscuit and juice to the kids. He said the Holy Rollers had very stirring tent meetings. They would go on for days getting worked up into a frenzy, talking in tongues, and such. The preachers would get very inspired and their sermons would become thunderous. He said there was a very common looking poor woman there one time, who got extremely ecstatic. She was talking in tongues, and he said it wasn't babble either. He could sense it was real. He somehow got too close to her and simply putting her hand on his shoulder, she turned him a flip, landing him flat on the floor. I don't know if that had any lasting effect on him. But, there were mystical things happening here in this family of his. I would come to find out about them years later, when I myself started meditating in my fifties.

He had gifts, as did others in his family. It was to my good fortune that these stories somehow started coming out of the woodwork too, because I could thus challenge his 'Good ol boy' facade when he would try to delude himself and my stand by saying such things as "there is no God, there's no such thing as reincarnation, meditation is silly", and the like. Yes, I have some ammunition now to stand up at least a little, for what I have been uncovering in my teachings, when the conversation wonders around into the unchartered territory of spirituality. I still don't wave the word "Guru" around, even though I am getting braver.

The odd thing is that he has had and still does intentionally have many experiences in his life that reveal these very truths in the most glorious ways. He does miraculous things but scoffs at the suggestion that such possibilities exist. For some reason he has fallen into some kind of (maybe karmically induced) denial. He has the kochas (veils) before his eyes, as Sri Yukteswargi would say. Like, after seeing his grandmother levitate a table with his own eyes, he will look straight at me and state "There's no such thing as levitation".
He was to be an extraordinary influence in my life though.

Maybe, could it be..I might have a role to play in instigating the uncovering of a treasure or two   for **him** too ?.. But, I do get ahead of myself..

I just had a realization; profound in its sudlty, about suffering. I think of it constantly. For, I have always been uncomfortable to some extent. I am trying to learn how to be tranquil so the anxiety can dwindle to a resting point.
Swamiji said something about a ballet dance performance he saw one time. The artist thought of himself as rather new age. Every time the dancers expressed themselves outwardly; or in some way outward from their centers, instead of resolving back, they would take that outside point as a new starting point and continue outward from there. It was intensely dissatisfying, as Swamiji put it. I think I have been doing this in my life. My daily work seems a torture to me for this reason. I drift out from the bosom of God, and the contentment of my spine, to do some outward action.
Then I get a little uncomfortable. But, I continue on without a check. I use where I've landed as a starting point to go further. I could go back if I could be intensely aware of needing to go back in the moment. But, I'm not tuned in that well as a rule. So, I begin a labyrinth of movement. My flow of energy starts to tie itself in knots going here and there. Maybe it's just the simple matter of move-go back, move-go back. Start from the original starting point each time; the center of the wheel instead of some point up one of the spokes. Then the rolling along is smooth, not bumpy.
When I find myself feeling uneasy, I will carefully trace it back to where it started. I will start there from a fresh blank page.
I will think "How does Master feel, this very moment" Then go there. Start from there. Maybe it will begin to come naturally.
Then, after you've found peace in meditation, use the method for each moment of life.
Thus Anandamayi Ma used to say "I am always the same".

ELEPHANT IN THE ROOM

If your karma was good enough to land you in Master's ashram in those early California days, you had a mighty force on your side. One time after warning the Monks not to hitch hike, one of them did and almost got forced into commiting a robbery. However, none of the inhabitants in the house heard the banging on the windows and the thieves were finally deterred and left.

Master scolded the Monk; uncovering his secret and declaring that he had to obstruct the hearing of all the people in that house!

Bobby said he was "turrible strong". When I met him at age 39, he could rip a yellow page telephone book in two, or press the full weight of a bathroom scale with his hands. He had such mastery over his energy. Even as a kid, he said he wasn't afraid of anybody. Ever! He could feel his strength, and could always tell that it excelled over whatever he was up against. He used to run up walls to the tops of buildings, and turn flips off of them. And he was always full of mischief and fun, pulling practical jokes, and laughing heartily. I noticed about him, that he took pleasure in the smallest of things. Like, the way a cat would play with something. Also, he had these little kind of slogans that became like mantras for him; things he would repeat often in fun, that made other people think he was rather simple. Like, if you mentioned something about somebody, he might say "you still like'im dontcha?" And you would have to answer "Yea". I was reminded hundreds of times that I liked our babies that way. Strange to say in spite of the repetition being tedious, it did start to place very positive affirmations on those souls within our sphere of attention. One time an old timer approached him on a scaffold laying bricks, and struck up a conversation with him, about how things have changed. Bob added "you know what I really miss.. the hoakey pokey." "What's that.."

Sticking out his leg and wiggling his hips he said "you know, ya putcher right foot in, ya putcher right foot out.." and proceeded to sing the hoakey pokey song." He said the old fella just kind of shook his head and walked off.

He also uses a technique he calls 'misdirection' in conversations where he wants someone's attention. If the subject is rather lofty and thinks you could miss the point, he'll put in a dumb word like 'atlisphere' instead of atmosphere, or something got 'tooken' instead of taken. He says that 'bump' conflicts with what had gotten too smooth and thus gets noticed. People like mistakes, and they'll listen intently to see how this intelligence conflicts with the absurd. He's got no pride.

But, in his head are whirling intricate scientific theories and the common denominators of everything that ticks. He can tell you the light years distance something is and how long it would take to get there in time, just off the cuff. He'll recite whole letters Lincoln wrote or statistics from the civil war. He recounts beautiful poetry from many different sources, even poetry he wrote himself. A delicate romantic heart lingered somewhere under that tall solid frame too. He told me that one time on a bus when he was about 21, he leaned over and kissed a girl on the back of her neck. Said he didn't realize he was gona do it till it was too late. I feel lucky when he pats me on the head. It's not much, but it's all in the eyes and it means a great deal to me. And, that's the kind of interaction he always had with his mom. She might knuckle his head under her arm, or reach out and touch his forehead, like you do to check for a fever. He said he would have gotten into a lot of trouble had it not been for her. He didn't want to bring any grief of any kind on her. She was a study in selfless service, resilience and sheer beauty of spirit. The door would open after 11 at night, and the kids would jump up to meet her coming home from the bus stop where she walked a mile after a double shift downtown in a hot restaurant kitchen. She had cornsticks and biscuits wrapped in a napkin in her pocket. Sometimes it was all they had to eat the whole day. She would curl her hair and go to bed, to rise at 4 and do that six days a week.

I knew her about fifteen years when she was in her 70's and 80's. She took a liking to me and kept a picture of me with one of my Uncle Chief's horses right by her bed on the wall. I sure did like her too. I was always amazed by her sweetness and composure. She was a shining light example to me. Being high strung as I was, it was just a pure relief to be around her. I never saw her angry.

In fact I never saw her without that certain twinkle in her eye. I was to realize what that was after I started on the path again, years after she died. I was to learn that she had meditated a good part of her adult years. I had no idea that I had been close to a meditater all that time. Bob told me rather reluctantly that she had sat in a chair for hours and "zoned out". We looked in her notes after she died and she had kept daytime schedules. She always dedicated an hour or more for "bliss". I know that between her two shifts at the kitchen, she had 3 hours off in which she had access to a board bed in a cellar. I am thinking this was her meditation bench, and she was able to spend that time with God, who gave her the energy she needed for the work she would endlessly and contentedly put out. She was slow and steady about things; plain and simple and never wanted for a single thing. She kept a garden and beautiful flowers in the yard. She always put a blessing into the food she cooked and it was the best I ever had; hard tack, beans, cornbread, turnip greens.

Her big offering was at Christmastime. She would start saving loose change throughout the year, and we would bring her our change pot at Thanksgiving time. She would roll up all the coins and spend them on food and little gifts for Christmas. As she lay dying after months of being bedridden, she softly woke that final morning to see her grown, indeed old children gathered around her bed. She inspiringly asked "is it Christmas?" "No Mama", said Wanda. " We're just visiting." She then left with an enchanted smile. This woman was Bob's hero. She had sometimes attended a Unity Church, the very affiliation Master spoke at when he first came to America. I wonder what she was able to glean from his spirit being on the planet, in the same country, at the same time as he was. She was a gentle loving spirit like he. She never complained. She was dharmic, even minded and cheerful. No wonder this boy Bobby was born to her. At a young age he realized that when you don't know something, instead of conjuring up an answer in your head, just open your mind instead and let the answer come in. He would answer questions about things he had never studied. He saw how things fit together, as he put it. He saw deep into scientific theories, and into the very minds of History's greatest characters.

 When he was old enough, he went to Viet Nam. Some of the things he experienced there he won't ever talk about even to me. He was out of a North Carolina paratrooper division. I know he learned some lessons there about obedience to authority figures, and he was put in solitary confinement for a good stretch. It was barely big enough to move in he said, and he was alone in there for many days. He kept his mind fresh by building a house. He started from scratch and just slowly built the whole thing. What captured my attention is how he described the process; he kept adding on to what he had already built, remembering every single portion. The structure that was supporting each new day's work was a lucid intricate picture in his mind, that he was able to maintain and build on.

Even now he has wonderful inventions waiting to be assembled. He says they will work too. One is a hovering lawn mower. Another is a totally new kind of transmission he's come up with in theory. One thing though, about Bob's personality, is that aside from being able to design, build or fix almost anything, he has this certain characteristic of stubbornness and won't compromise. As a brick layer, for example, he is able to make beautiful medieval style interlaced brick patterns, herringbone designs, arches etc. But many times, people won't ask for his expertise or opinion, and he remains quiet. He also won't argue. One time a man he was working for came while he was setting his line, and said it didn't look square. "It's square", Bob said. "I believe it should be here", said the man pointing to a different spot. Bob said not another word and built the whole wall from that measurement. It was then more than obvious how crooked it was. He had to tear the whole thing down. But, he wasn't going to argue. I have learned from these kinds of experiences to grab the nugget when it is offered from him, and don't miss the chance.

He is very yogic in his focus, as well as his strength. You would see if you were around him, that in any thoughtful exchange his reply is right on the money. It is given of right motives, is clever, and usually the most astute answer available. You can't confuse him. Thoughts are universal, and he is able somehow to access the right one immediately. Thus, he is king of the clever comeback. You may get the last word, but he gets the best one!

And too, he has the uncanny ability of attracting what he wants. He somehow knows not to use this power selfishly, but if it is for a generous purpose, he can manifest things, manipulate circumstances, or simply bring someone immediately into his camp.

If you are already suffering a great deal in life, then trying to achieve enlightenment could be kind of like making a dire run for cover. Let's say it's 80 below in the arctic, and you're in an igloo. Cold, clammy.. You're dying in that igloo. But, there's a warm cabin with a fire miles up the trail. By the grace of God, you now know for a certainty that the cabin is there. But you also know it is locked. You can make a run for it, but you'll have to figure out a way to jimmy that lock, in that weather. You study what you know about locks, but you have no idea what you will encounter. But you believe if you take the time and effort to figure out that locking system, and fail to master it, you will be too compromised by the cold to go all the way back to the igloo. So it's the cabin or freeze. You have to try for the better life. You make a run for it and get there, and you are starting to succumb to the elements. You are not used to them. Concentrating is grueling. But, with the pressure is the greatest of incentive. Never will you give up and die-- You have come this far! You finally steady yourself, pick the lock with calm certainty and a will of steel, and you enter in, forever. Oh, you will have to fix the cabin up, but the heat is on, and you're in.

Up in the Yukon, among the dog-sled racers, there's a saying; "If you're not the lead dog, your view will never change." In the darkness of meditation, you gotta swell out ahead and above all of the mental citizens milling about; wishing, scheming, procrastinating.. and get right in there. I mean business. I am working for Master! He has put his trust in my strength and ability. And, I can maintain all the weight the job entails, and maneuver around all the obstacles. This work is for all of us; all of Master's family, and he has entrusted me with it. I'll do it just the way he would!

I am well able to work for all the other children, for I have been practicing and am getting so much stronger. The darkness and uncertainty of this area tries to swerve me off my course. Ha, I am used to it. It's like home to me because there is a joyous love all around in here, I've learned how to gain access to. Amazing, but it's been here the whole time. It's starting to seep into my being the more I come in here. I pull the whole environment close in to myself where I can do my work meticulously, and please Master. It is just my love, this wonderful job. And I feel the fizzling warmth of success start to vibrate my heart, spreading throughout my body. Not long and I'll be there at the finish with you Sir. Just around the corner. Another good days work!

THE WINTER OF OUR DISCONTENT

After he came home from Viet Nam, he got a motorcycle and headed out to California. He was full of vim and vigor and, having read the Grapes of Wrath by Steinbeck and having been impressed by the cast and California in the Hollywood movie of it, he struck out with great inspiration to see this part of the country along route 66. He had a fanciful notion too, about marrying the daughter of film producer John Huston; actress, Angelica Huston. In Nashville he had been a sought after conversationalist around the music row writers of the day. So thought provoking were his ideas about things, that folk artists like Janis Ian, and Kris Kristoferson were always happy to run into him. He always however, wore short hair and never donned any hippy garb. (So he was the one who stood out from the crowd. Ironically, that's what the hippies were trying to do.)

In California, he got many odd jobs. As it turned out, and I didn't know till a few years ago, he realized there that he had the ability to heal people. They didn't have to believe or anything like that. He just had to be able to get his hands on them, and they were healed. It did take something out of him, and sometimes he would be left fatigued or slightly injured himself. And too, he would "lose time" and kind of blank out for a period of time. But this practice finally ran him out of California and back home where he learned not to make mention of such things. People were after him all the time, and it got wearisome for him.

But his experience of California was worthy of a book in itself. What an "Americana in the 60's" story. Steinbeck himself couldn't have wrung out of that great state any grander adventures. He was a short order cook in little way side cafés. He was a ranch hand, a mechanic, a gas station attendant.. he spent nights in ditches and woke up going any direction he felt like. He hobo'd on trains. He studied the land to its very essence. Not only California did he explore. He went all over.

We were watching "The Unforgiven" one night, and Clint Eastwood said "I thought I was in hell but I woke up and I was only in Nebraska". Bob sat back and mused into those days again, saying "I was working there for an old man and his sister. They had hundreds of acres of land they farmed, and their family had for three generations back. He told me one day that I could have it all if I would stay. I thought I had hit heaven. But, it began to lay heavy on me, as day after day stretched on under bent shoulders; milking cows, gathering eggs, cleaning barns and coops, forever gathering rocks that the frost had loosened, and carrying them to the fence lines, fixing fences. I moved from the barn into the house during the bleak stark winter. There was frost on the backs of the cattle, even in the barn. There was no TV, no radio. We sat in front of the fire and spoke only once in awhile. Come spring when it was finally warm enough to put it out on the road, I jumped on my bike a free man. That had been a scary prospect. That land would have owned me, not me it. I'd have had to spend the next fifty some odd years trying to find somebody to hand it off to." He said.

In Montana one time he fell asleep in a boxcar, and the train sidetracked him in the middle of nowhere. He woke up and walked to the highest hill he could find to look around. There was absolutely nothing but prairie all around as far as the eye could see. No road, just a little stream far off. He started to walk but realized that may be a path of no return, so decided to take his fate back to the boxcar and wait. It was close to a week before the train came back for the boxcar. He said he well knew how to make a snare for rabbits, but opted instead to just eat some grasses and bark he knew to have nutrition. He remembers, when we hear James Taylor singing Sweet Baby James, sitting around a fire all by himself in some remote place, kinda wishing he was in a tavern somewhere with someone to talk to.

He had some rather disturbing incidents back then too. He went to work for a man who had two sons on a ranch. The man belittled the boys and beat them for no reason at all it seemed to Bob.

The first time he tried to speak in that manner to Bob though, he stated "Whoa, you don't speak that way to me. I'm a human being just like you are. I won't have it." And the man gave a wide birth to this young man. But one day they were out in the yard, and the old man grabbed one of his sons by the ear, heaving him right off the ground. Bob grabbed an axe handle and broke the man's legs. He left without his pay. He had hair trigger reactions to things. He delved out instant karma. One time he was at a gathering where a guy belched loudly as he walked by Bob, and he threw the guy right out of the nearby second story window, through the pane and all.

He got to see the country on his terms, and at a gloriously free time in his life. After he returned to Tennessee, he had gotten married, had a son, and began a life of hard work and family obligations.

I met him years later. He was sitting with his back to the wall in a little divey bar I played in on weekends. It was in the neighborhood he lived in. He was wary of people, and it seemed to me he was rather a dark character. But, we got to talking, and within a few weeks he had written some poetry for me. Within a year I had bought my first house. It was badly in need of repair and he totally renovated it, making it a very deluxe little dwelling. He didn't even want any pay. Bob was intelligent like my dad, but what was also so endearing for me, was that he reminded me of the Quintal boys, and I was so lonesome for home. The mundane world of men and machines was just what I needed to get my head to stop reeling over the music business pressures, and my personal misfortunes. Oh, for life to just be simple again. I didn't know what a deep soul he was. This revelation was a slow one, unraveling in the twenty years that passed.

Shortly after our son was born, in the early 90's, Bob started having anxiety attacks. They got so bad, that they took him out of life in a way. They broke him. It was heart breaking. Sometimes he couldn't leave the house; this man who had been so brave. He was so ashamed. He would have spells where he was suddenly so tortured by anxiety, that we would have to go home right then, even in a restaurant. I saw this condition take my husband slowly from me. No one ever knew but me. He started thinking about God, and he decided there wasn't one. Mark Twain had gotten cynical near the end of his life, and Bob felt akin to the quotes he would often recall from Twain's last very pessimistic book called "Letters from the Earth".

In fact, here let me detour somewhat to include some quotes Bob has clung to throughout his life. They cast a great deal of insight into the reasons this boy who experienced so much social cruelty, would turn his attention to the deep recesses of hopelessness. He was onto something here; pinning down the purpose of life, but the answers were yet to be clear. Delusion can so closely masquerade truth. Engaging thoughts indeed though, are the following;

AurthurMiller; Death of a Salesman;

"Above all perhaps was a need greater than hunger, thirst or sex—a need for immortality; a need to leave a thumbprint somewhere in the world and by admitting it, the knowing that one has carefully inscribed his name on a cake of ice on a hot July day."

"The image of aging and so many of your friends already gone and strangers in the seats of the mighty, who do not know you or your triumphs or your incredible value- the image of a private man in a world full of strangers. A world that is not home or even an open battleground; but only galaxies of high promise over a fear of falling."

"The image of the sun's hard public eye upon you, no longer swept by your myth; no longer rousable from his separateness, no longer knowing you have lived for him and have wept for him."

The hard times Bob had seen as a boy had begun to twist his perception of God. He delved deep into delirious writings that were very convincing. He even began to wonder if God had fixed it to where you couldn't escape even **after** death. (Well, we know it's true on certain levels, but not in the way outlined in these subsequent paragraphs.) Some of the ideas that began to captivate him even back then, were thus;

"The deities saw that death was an admirable agent in inflicting pain on the living. But it let the dead person get away scott free in the blessed refuge of the grave. So, he invented Hell and proclaimed it.

This was Mark Twain's natural progression from the thought

"All of us have to suffer the slings and arrows of outrageous fortune. Life was no valuable gift but death was. Life was a fever dream of joys embittered by sorrows and pleasures poisoned by pain.

But, death was sweet. Death was gentle and kind. It healed a bruised spirit and a broken heart and gave a man rest and forgetfulness. When a man could endure life no longer, death came and set him free."

(I feel, my dear that you are closer to the truth if you put the word God in the places where death is written.)

(Remember what Shakespear said, that you loved;)

"To be or not to be. That is the question. To shuffle off this mortal coil; to die, to sleep, to dream. BUT, therein lies the rub; for what dreams may come.."

(dreams indeed, all)

He wanted to die, and he was hoping there was nothing but blessed rest past the grave. I was in shock, with two young teenagers, trying to hold down a job and keep us going. He had always held me up, and what about **my** depression; an onslaught that was never very far from me on any given day. I was desperate. I had started going to church some years before. Protestant religions were very strange in some ways to me. I just didn't know what to think of some of it.

One day at my job the thought popped into my head "I wonder if Swami Kriyananda is still alive".

That's what started it. Within a few months I had totally embraced the teachings of Yogananda. This time for real. It has changed my life so completely, that I have written various letters trying to describe my elation. If I hadn't done that when the spirit hit me, I feel the very rocks would have had to cry out. One of these letters, then, may suffice to shed some light on my feelings around that time.

There was a girl.

She was raised up in a remote farming community on the prairies of Northwestern Canada, above the magnificent Banff and Jasper Rocky Mountains. She was wondrously contented by nature in its beauty, and exploring helped her to forget how alien she otherwise felt with the people of this world.

By her early fifties, she had anxiety. Her husband seemed not to want to live. He had trouble leaving the house, and had physical ailments. She became profoundly sad and worried about her family with its 2 young teenagers. She cried about many things, like the sufferings of animals. She wrote a statement one day that said; "Life is the ongoing succession of each inconvenient event --without which would render it totally monotonous."

One day at her job, a spiritual teacher she had read of in her 20's popped into her head. She googled him and he appeared on her screen. She dove into his teachings. She started to feel a trickling of divine truth and peace into her heart. She grew to love the saint so much that she voyaged to see him and received a blessing from him. She wrote songs for him, and wrote him letters. He answered some of them.

Her meditations became blessed too, with the warm vibrant love she felt for him. Deep within she felt as a flower opening up to the sun. He was so beautiful. More and more she trustingly let go to him. More and more she carried love into her day and deep into the nights, chanting his name and singing his songs in her heart.

Finally one day she realized that her husband had fallen deeply in love with her. He had great strength, not unlike his younger days. His poetry and intuition came back. He had no fear and knew the right thing to do in every situation. His touch began to heal people and he had wonderful inventions in his head. Her children were giving her hugs for no reason. Their eyes glowed. Her home was a sanctuary of peace, and good fortune followed her.

One night her husband had a dream that he would have to fight an opponent for her love. But he grew to like the opponent so much that instead, he invited him to come and live with them. She felt like the saint had become part of her family and her soul. She wasn't ever sure though, if he **could** even pick her out of a crowd

GIFTED

Bob seemed to be getting better after I started meditating. Maybe it was because I was clearer, and could help him. Being around someone being uplifted, helped to uplift him too I bet. During some of his darkest times, however, he had embarked on a journey that was ongoing even now. In the depths of his delirium, he had created a path to lead him out of the labyrinth. When he wanted to go home so badly, he started directing his dreams until he found a road he could get on that led to a crossroad. He thought his ma might be over the hill there, and his brother Jimmy, who had died. He longed to see them and to rest. He never has gone over that hill though. It occurs to him that to do that might mean he won't see me and the kids again. He never did get quite that desperate.

But a manifestation of joy came to him there at those crossroads, in the form of a young man; a carefree sort rolling a cigarette under the shade of a big sycamore tree. Was he a man of Bob's making? Possibly. He was just the kind of guy Bob liked, Bob **was** in fact. Somewhat like the older fellows who would gather around the town square whittling and talking amongst themselves when he was a boy. He had on overalls, and he was intelligent and soft spoken. In Bob's dreams this man became recognizable as the character 'Tom Joad' from the 'Grapes of Wrath', played by Henry Fonda. So began an extraordinary friendship that goes on to this day.

Bob started going to Tom to ask questions that plagued him in his everyday life. Inexplicably he would just direct himself to go there in these lucid dreams, after he fell asleep at night. His health started improving and he was starting to be his old self. He had been going for some time before he ever mentioned it to me that he had been "intentional dreaming" this way.

One morning he went to the bathroom, and coming out, thought "It's 4:44 in the morning". He looked at the clock and it was.

This reminded him of something about numbers. Climbing back into bed, he remembered he had been talking to Tom. It was a beautiful day at the crossroads, and Bob could see all the colors so vividly. He remembered the bright red of the handkerchief tied around Tom's neck, the richness of the soil, and he even remembered the smell of the Bull Durham tobacco Tom was rolling up with one hand. "What's on yer mind, boy?" Tom had asked. A little embarrassed to be vacant minded, Bob scrambled to come up with something. "Why not give me the lottery numbers if you know em." Tom's head fell back in laughter. "Hell, boy is that all you want? Here." And he proceeded to rattle off 5 numbers. Bob thought of writing them down. Then, certain he would remember, he opted not to. Resting on the edge of the bed, Bob had sat up to tell me about knowing the time without looking. Then he told me the rest of the story as he had been reminded of it.

I was floor boarded. "What are the numbers?" I asked. He started to recite them, but only remembered three. Darn it, he continued. I should have written them down. He remembered a fourth, and then guessed at a fifth. I was so amazed at this "going where you want in your dream" business, that I determined to check this out. Later that day I played the numbers at the local convenience store. That night we watched on tv while 4 of them came in. The 3 he knew, and the fourth, but I had put it in the wrong place. It was supposed to be the power ball number. The number we needed was the missing one. If we hadn't been the ones to experience this, we'd never have believed it. We did win a prize. But we were never to be the same after this event. Both of us knew on some deep level, that there was more to this experience than meets the eye.

We don't play the lottery

Someone was trying to tell us something.
....

One of the conversations between Bob and Tom yielded this information; "when you hear the names Mallory and Malloy, then you'll know the world 'as we know it' will be about to end. ✷

✷
A note of interest here. It is many months after the prediction Tom Joad gave Bob about Mallory and Molloy. This book is about to go to print today 11-23-10. And, yesterday, Bob told me he was taking Nathan to the college, and noticed--stopped at a light beside him was a big wrecker truck that said "Molloy" road as an address. He peeked up and under the window it said "Mallory" as the owner. The driver caught his glance, and smiling, gave him a little salute. He had on a flat looking hat just like Toms. So i wonder what it all means...

Bob was asking practical questions of Tom, but sometimes the conversation would go its own way. Bob began to shy away from visiting Tom. He didn't know how to deal with phenomena like this, and wanted only a simple life. Tom had also explained one time about the concept of parallel universes being perfectly reasonable. How space could bend, like with heat from the gravitational pull of a star. Like a fabric, it could be bent and fold over, making the distance shorter between two points, and at the point where the fabric touched in its overlap, both places could have the same thing happening at once. They also discussed things like the super collider where light had been stopped in mid air.

The fact that Bob comprehended these concepts, and was absorbed into them, was a bit much for him. Realities came to his mind that he wasn't willing to consider. It overwhelmed him. He began to go less and less. I told him to ask Tom about reincarnation, but he didn't bother to do it. I always thought it quite interesting though; Steinbeck having lived in California at the time Master was there, giving the line to Tom Joad " We are all part of one big soul, one consciousness."

Bob also said that he knew his Ma was there at those crossroads, just over the hill, and his intuition told him that if he tried to see her, he would die because it would be so peaceful he wouldn't be able to make himself leave then. It was all unsettling for him. So a time went by when he didn't visit there. Then came the BP oil disaster in the Gulf. Bob kept telling me "I know there's a way to cap that leak. I'm going to figure it out." I could see he was deeply pondering this in the days to come. Finally he said "I'm going to ask Tom". A couple days later he announced "I know how to do it. I asked Tom, and he said you could use a concept similar to what John Roebling did to construct those huge feet for the Brooklyn Bridge." "But, you already know that, don't you Bob." Bob smiled. "Yea, float those big concrete caseons out there upside down, with piping on the corners to adjust the air levels, keeping it float balanced. Have wedged walls on the thing so when you flip it over, the wedges will dig into the sea bottom. Then float it over-top the spill, turn it over, and guide it down. You can then use the piping to pour concrete down and fill it up. It would be good to have robars in there too.

Just fill it all up with the concrete, and then concentrate on building the new pipe. For that matter, he continued in his thought, you may even be able to use an upside down barge in much the same way." Well, we thought it was a good idea, but I emailed various news stations, and I don't guess anyone else thought it was.

Just the other night in fact, he was back to visit Tom after not going for some time. He has been having somewhat of a fascination with old tractors, and fixing them out in the yard. Now he has an old BMW car out there, and the gas tank had been unusable because of what had gotten all sludged up inside it. I went out onto the side deck to shake a rug, and heard a clug-clug-clugging sound. I looked over and saw the gas tank rotating round and round off the jacked up wheel of one of Bob's tractors in gear. It was secured on there with bunji chords and there was the sound of rocks and gravel clanging around inside scraping it clean.

I looked astonished over at Bob tinkering with an engine in the yard, and with a wide grin he looked over his shoulder at me and hollered "I bin to see Tom!"

Not just this friendship with Tom is curious, but everything that happens around this man. People make excuses to visit him, and very often say they feel so much better afterwards. Confusion and even ill feelings are quickly diminished in his presence. He gets phone calls from an array of new and old acquaintances asking his advise on anything, or some specific fact they need verified. Even if they're just playing Trivial Persuit, and wondering about something, it's like the game Jeopardy. He can watch that show and rattle off every answer.
People will talk to him too, about sensitive heart-felt matters of concern. He'll casually offer some uplifting, off-the-wall logical fact that will hit the nail right on the head for them, and set them back on track. His advice on a situation is the last word for many. You can sense from him a genuine experience of knowing something. His offering is always understated and matter of factly given. Many times I will be consumed by some problem, and he will state something simply that makes it disappear. It might not even have had anything to do with what was on my mind. But, he put his attention there for me and erased it with his mis-direction. Last year I had planned a vacation for me, the kids, and their friends to the mountains of Gatlinberg. He was

concerned the car was too old, and was worried for our safety and comfort. A couple days before we left, home he came with a beautiful Hyundai Santa Fe. It was a $12,000 vehicle but he could only come up with 6 and got it anyway. I had a speeding ticket he worried about, and said he'd try to fix. He made a call and it was gone. These kinds of things happen all the time. People will start to talk business with him, and suddenly just smile engagingly. The next thing you know they're offering him the kitchen sink. He doesn't care about money or owning things though. He just waits till something is needed and simply makes it happen. Many people have remarked that he is the most amazing man they have ever met; even people that haven't been around him much. The ones that have are devoted to him.

Bob was reluctant, but finally one day, he told me about being able to heal people. He wanted to help his friend with brain cancer, but wasn't able to get to him in time. He worried about explaining to sick people wanting to touch them, but the urge to help was coming back to him with his better health, and he admitted to me that it was something he was able to do. In fact, pieces started fitting together in my mind, for I knew how he could sway all kinds of situations his way. I don't know why he got so sick for all those years himself. He knew how to swerve around such things. He had, I started to remember, touched me many times, and some onslaught or another I had been experiencing would stop. One day I noticed a big age spot by my eye. After about a month it grew a black uneven bump on it, that looked very ominous. I was worried about it. In bed one night I felt a spark on that side of my face. I asked Bob the next day if he had touched it. Yes. Within a couple days it was gone. Last month, I had a breast exam, and was called back in a hurry when they saw something suspicious. I was pretty nervous about it, as family members have had breast cancer. I told Bob about the test. He stood behind me and put his hands to my chest. It made him feel faint, and even hurt his shoulder. He said "did you feel that bolt". I hadn't really. He had to sit for a spell. But the next morning my breast exam was perfectly normal. The nurse tried to explain it away as something they only thought they saw, but she looked quite surprised. Bob laughed, " I even tried it on a car" Robert had asked him to come and get his car going in the driveway. He had tried all he knew to do. Bob said "I just got the thought to walk up to it and put my hand on it. I felt a jolt.

Suddenly I realized I had lost time, and had been standing there dazed. I went and turned the key in the ignition and she started like a top. "

Not long ago, I asked him "Did your mom have this gift?" Well, he said, she was always reaching to touch my forehead..always. We never had health care. But none of us ever got a sickness".

"Could you feel that it worked every time you did it?" No he said. Once when Dude; his mother's husband was near the end of his life, and came on the jobsite rundown and very sickly, Bob felt mercy for him. He had been a brute; had mistreated animals, and had behaved very badly most of his life. Bob said "I just didn't want to see him suffer. But, when I put my hand on him, he was just ", he paused ."Dead?" I asked. "Well", Bob went on.. "I felt nothing there I could work with. He was just **mean**".

Have you been healing much of the time we've known each other? I inquired. "Remember when Pop had cancer about 15 years ago?" "That's right". I said." It disappeared". "Have you or the kids ever been sick?" he asked "No. Neither has your son Robert." Bob smiled.

Strange, this world of Bobby Crowell, wouldn't you say..

Well, my dear Bob, I can't help but wonder what could have been had you met Swami Kriyananda in California back then. What a comfort you could have been to him, and what a help. Oh, you would have balked at the spiritual talk at first. But, you would have thrived on being needed in a practical way. You would have found great condolence in being able to build his dome structures and publications building roof, fix his car when it would throw a rod, invent alternative power sources for the work.. You could even have given healing touches when he worked too hard and manifested sickness. Then, slowly you would have begun to glean from the great Saint, grasping his concepts easily, and he yours. Yes, Swamiji would have won you over. Even in your dream, you grew quickly to love him instead of perceiving him as your opposition. He would have adored your humble nobility. But, instead of him harnessing your greatness and ingenuity, Master let you go back to Tennessee and prepare for one day when you would find a scared little rabbit who had become entangled in a fence, trying to get into the garden, and was dying there.

How fortunate I am, my dearest Bob, that you have been my friend all these years. How I love to sit with you immersed in conversation, amazed by your intelligence and sensibilities. I think you have been a mighty warrior in other lifetimes. But more than that, you have realized great heights in many ways. I am so honored to have been this near to you.

For, you were the one the Masters sent in answer to my desperate cry at the laundry mat, to stop the spiraling confusion that needed immediate attention in this world of my creation-- that was suffocating me. You would settle my jittering nerves and stop my incessant outward thrusting in life. No longer would I keep looking for answers way out in the seas of uncertainty. You brought everything in close. We sat at home. I no longer felt compelled to rush about following whims. We lived a structured life, a normal life. I wanted only finally, to please my family, and settled in to doing good work. How long had I waited for this good karma to kick in, I don't know. But when the 3000 miles were closed between us, here you were waiting in the wings, my very own husband for this lifetime. With your guidance, I could finally prepare and refine myself enough to recognize Master behind the scenes. I would begin to tame my restlessness enough to make an effort toward him and my final pathway.

I often wonder, was my state of mind the toxic catalyst that brought on the onslaught of that terrible sickness you endured for all those years? Well, that karma is behind you now. You have conquered it. And look what it has done for me. It was suffering through that very sickness of yours that thrust me to the depths, grasping for my God. That is when he answers you. Not until.

 Oh, Bob, we are two happy children, aren't we..Lets get out of this tall grass. I hope against hope that before this life is over, you'll wake up my teacher, to know what you have taught.

This morning after my kriyas, I paused before going into the Hong Sau technique. I felt blanketed in a shroud of love, drawn from my spine upward toward Master. I was tinkering a bit with the thought "who am I, really? Or, where does this idea of 'I' come from?" I know that if I stay with this thought, it will start to creep into the woodwork of these old walls of flesh and find its point of conception. It may not spark much of a response right now, but I have experienced how staying with something can bring results. Every day now for many months I have dedicated the length of a song at work, to Master. When a particularly beautiful song comes into my headphones, I stop all I am doing and look into his eyes in my favorite picture of him. At first I had to concentrate a bit to keep the focus there, but it didn't take long until I was drawn to settle into the pool of love within those lustrous eyes. Now it is a refreshing, deeply soothing experience. There is so much expression there, and I get inklings of what he feels for me. This practice has born beautiful results too, in that I feel him closer in my life and my meditations, and I am developing such a deep longing for him.

So, I know to keep with this new question, and it will bring results too. I was tempted at first to think "I won't get a result from this. I am not developed far enough along to penetrate into such a question." No! That is *not* the way to think. I have realized I must always say yes to life. I have seen now, time and time again, how amazing perceptions have manifested slowly and surely within my dedication for him. This is no different. When my distractions come, I think "What would Master do?" Of course he would not bother giving any energy to the distraction. So, let it go. Simple. Go back with my practice.

And, when I am drawn ever deeper in my feeling of love for Master, I want to get right inside him. That way I can share his consciousness. Would he not love it if I advanced enough to be able to share his bliss, the way Saint Lynn did? I know he is my father, and so I can get up on his lap and try driving, as it were. He lets me take the wheel. And, he is pleased when I not only try driving, but I use the opportunity to sneak right inside him. Again, if it is hazy, I won't think "I can't do this". Instead, I just go on, venturing deeper into his being. Already I feel a wondrous expansion within and without; a feeling of being somehow close to home. It may be for just a fleeting moment or two right now, but I will just keep trying in my meditations. One day I will feel deeply the love that is in him, and it will be part of all that is, and I will become that.

DREAM A LITTLE DREAM OF ME

When I was little, I remember once having a euphoric experience. I think I had the flu, and right before I woke up sick, I had been ecstatic. The graphics of this experience seemed really to have nothing to do with the feelings of it. I was a little kid, so they may have been something I'd noticed around me at the time. I know my mom was always playing cards with little groups of people and it was always a happy occasion. Well, there was this queen of hearts card sitting on a pin (maybe there was a little Alice in Wonderland in there too..) All the other cards were flat on the floor uniformly placed, and all was calm; serenely so. It was a feeling of perfect bliss. I could have felt this forever. However, the cards started to curl up at the edges (as if wet or something). This brought tremendous disharmony to my little scene. A roller; like a steam roller or big rolling pin, came in to roll over the cards to flatten them once more. This agitated me so greatly that I woke up needing to throw up, and I became very sick, for days. Maybe I was remembering the astral world, and how while being there, I had started becoming restless again, and would be forced to leave that world and return to the gross one. I was devastated at having to leave; literally sickened.

And too, as a little girl, I used to get the sensation that the dense material world would only appear at whatever scene scope was within the vision of my eyes at any given time. If I would look the other way, what I had been looking at would disappear and the world manifested fresh with the new direction. It was like it manifested for my eyes and experience only.

Well, when I started meditating in my early fifties, strange things also started to happen then. I tend to think that starting on the sincere path like that brings some good karma; a sort of promise of what is to come if one will stay with it. I had a few of these experiences.*

*
These novice experiences too, can be thought of like 'beginner's luck'. There are no thwarting cross currents of built up doubt because there is yet to be any perception of odds. So, a little horse who especially likes to run, can come in out of the pasture and win the Kentucky Derby.

I hadn't been meditating long when one night in bed I intruded on Swamiji. He was startled a bit. It was much more real than a dream had ever been. Almost scarily so. Swamiji knew I wasn't spiritually ready for such a visit. He said to me "But,.. you're sleeping". I thought very adamantly "No, I'm not. I'm really here". Then came an earth shaking vibration that was way out of my league, and I was literally shaken awake.

Soon after that experience came another one like it. I woke up wanting so passionately to meditate, that I jumped right into my spiritual eye, and the jolt caused a small cataclysm. Thunder hit so hard, that it shook right through me. I almost woke up, and then remembered that I wasn't sleeping..I was in meditation. I thought urgently to myself "You can do this!..just relax. Focus.. take it easy. I went down on one knee amidst the thunder. I became excited thinking about the barrier I may be able to cross here. It surely would be a short cut to some deeper level of realization if I could pull this off. I was perched for success. Then I got tricked. It popped into my head that it may start raining and I would get wet. I forgot it was cosmic thunder. I prepared to run for cover. That interrupted my scene. I popped out of it and realized I was indoors. It was too late to resume my experience. Looking outside, however, I didn't see a cloud in the sky.

Next I started dreaming of Master. In my first dream of him he was distant and I couldn't really get near him. He was kind of in a mist. Then one day I was inspired to write a song for Swamiji. It's called 'Kriyananda'. I worked on it very intensely to get it right, and I appealed to Master quite steadily throughout the process, seeking his approval; for somehow it was he initiating the writing of the song. Then, that night Master came into my dream, and he this time, came close enough for me to touch. He seemed pleased, and I was reminded of the time Sri Yukteswar let Master sleep in his bed after working so hard and selflessly, winning his guru's loving approval. Master was letting me lay down with him.

I was a bit awkward with this. I think I should have touched his feet. Instead, I did what came naturally to me, and put my arm across his belly in a kind of hug. He instantly turned into vast expanse of ocean.

Some months later I was preparing to be initiated onto the path. I was very earnestly studying my lessons and trying to live right in every way. I had a dream one night, that a bunch of us were at my cousin Vickie's grandmother; Gertie's house, where I'd spent many playful hours as a kid. She was perhaps the most pious woman I had known well. In fact once when I was very young; preschool, and wondering down the road, I was so longing to go to church, that I decided I could just walk in. I remember it was an Easter Sunday, and we didn't get to go to church. But, mom had after all, dressed me in what I thought was my nicest whitest sweater. That was my Sunday best, so I parlayed right in, proceeding to walk down the aisle toward the priest conducting the service. It was Gertie who had snatched me, and sat me with her, instructing me on the rituals and answers to be given.

Her house inside, I'd always considered as holy. Nine kids had been raised there to love God, and such a grand loving old house it was. So, back to the story. Here a bunch of us were in the dream, at Gertie's door, and who should come peering out of the screen but Master. Then he departed. I intuitively knew he was looking for me, and that I needed an offering. I became flushed, hurriedly looking around for a decent offering. I quickly gathered together some things we were carrying with us; camping gear..some blankets, utensils, and such. Then I remembered having gone to the store and getting a bag of potatoes. (That had happened in recent real life, not the dream.) Returning from the store and looking in the pantry I had seen I already had a bag. I know I had been a little concerned that one bag would go bad before all of them got used. Well, here in this dream, appeared my extra bag of potatoes, and I quickly added them to the offering, of all silly things.

Time was short, and sure enough Master appeared at the door again. He looked at the gathering of stuff in the yard, then shifted his gaze to me. This was my moment; my offering. This was me wanting so badly to be his.

Well, I blurted out something. I don't remember what the words were, but I remember the earnestness and desperation. Then, he smiled. I woke up. Within a week or so, I was at a little park in my car, conducting my own private initiation. I had my cd, and I was listening and repeating my dedication lines. I had picked wild flowers and had a check on the dashboard to send to Ananda. These were my offerings. I felt peaceful and pure. After the little ceremony, I walked out into the hills and joy flooded my heart, remembering Master at the screen door, and my real offering, for I knew in my very heart, that I had passed his test, and had been accepted into the inner light. My life was saved.

I MEANT to do my work today—
But a brown bird sang in the apple tree,
And a butterfly flitted across the field,
And all the leaves were calling me.

And the wind went sighing over the land,
Tossing the grasses to and fro,
And a rainbow held out its shining hand—
So what could I do but laugh and go?

RICHARD LE GALLIENNE

One morning I was in the midst of waking up, as it was time to get up. However, I was still looming pleasantly in my inspirations, and I became consciously aware of an ecstatic state I was in. It became more and more enthralling until it brought kundalini awakening. I was simply working in a kitchen in the olden days, at least I think I may have been working. I was just so content that love was pouring in and out of every pore in me. It was dark, the room was small, and the walls were piney, but a yellowish color.

I may have been baking bread. I don't ever remember being so very happy. Then suddenly I felt the stirring. I must have known what it was, for I braced myself against the wooden table.

Then like a fireball being shot from the bottom of my spine, right up through the top of my head, I surrendered to the most beautiful surge of energy. It thrilled my whole body into ecstasy as I vibrated there. After that, I felt like I was floating for much of the next week or so. I remember doing nothing to bring it on. It came of itself. It was its own thrust of happiness, of deep love.   I was just the channel it chose to free itself.

As Master had been so supportive in the writing of my little Kriyananda song, I decided to send it to Swami Kriyananda. Some time later I was elated to receive a very gracious response from him in the mail. He suggested I come to Ananda, and he would of course be there in the summer. Wow..why hadn't that ever occurred to me. Yes, I sure could go to Ananda couldn't I. I had actually become very reclusive, hardly ever travelling anymore, and I had anxieties. But, I had never been to California, ever.

And, this suggestion was from the one in this world who meant so much to me. I made arrangements to go to Spiritual Renewal week in September. As the date came closer, I became more and more blessed with meditative rewards for making such an effort. In my waking hours though, I worried how I might approach the great Swami. For, I so wanted his blessing. To be in the company of a Saint for even a moment can be your raft over the ocean of delusion. My inner enemies started to riddle me with self doubt. How will you approach such a being? You are a coward. You are of such a nervous type that your hands shake in plain sight. Never mind, I thought, clinging to my higher perceptions in meditation. Then one night Master came to help me.

In my dream I was in a big mall. My family lived off one of the doorways along the mall corridor, and I was out in it amidst all the people. Then my senses started tingling. I knew in an instant that Yogananda was in the building. And, he was quickly approaching. I looked over to my left. There, walking briskly with his head down was a fellow in a raincoat with the collar up, looking indistinct. It was him.

What was I to do? He urged me intuitively that now was it. This was my only chance. I hurried over to him and strode to keep up. I got his attention. He stopped and sharply looked at me. I almost faltered as I had with the bees. Then, I plunged helplessly into this opportunity, for I knew no other way. I blurted out "Yogananda" and somehow greeted him. His guard was instantly let down and my test had been passed. He actually embraced me. Then he spoke to me in a language I didn't know. Another test. Where I would usually just politely nod and try to somehow withdraw myself from the situation, I suddenly realized this kind of reasoning was not the right response. In fact, reasoning was not needed at all. Humility was. I instead for the first time, put myself in the vulnerable position of inquiry; knowing I was placing myself in the position of looking a fool if I wouldn't be able to further understand.

This was something I had been neglecting to do all my life, and it was causing me to miss out on the very essence and understanding of life itself. Now I desperately wanted to be a worthy student. I said "Pardon me, what was that Sir?" He was pleased. And then we understood each other. I was so overjoyed to be in his company, that I started reverting to the restlessness innate in me. I brought him into the dwelling of my family. I was nervous introducing him. I thought maybe I should entertain him in some way. Should I sing? What should I do? I became so restless that he had to opt out, but did so very graciously. Before he disappeared he disguised himself with a rusty colored corn roll type hair style, sat on the floor, put his head down..and he was gone.

I was saddened that he left. But upon waking, realized what a great blessing had been visited me.

Almost halfway through my stay at Ananda, I was realizing how impossible it was to get close to Swami Kriyananda. After his talks in the big beautiful outside amphitheatre, he was quietly ushered away.

You could hear a pin drop, and everyone's attention was keenly on him. There had been a couple occasions, however, where visitors approached him and he gave them blessings by placing his finger on their foreheads. They seemed so at ease with him. Why couldn't I be like that? Wednesday evening his wonderful play "The Peace Treaty" was being performed, and he was a little more relaxed as, he only was required to be an audience member and enjoy this night.

During the intermission a couple of teenage girls approached him for a greeting. He stood to bless them. After they left, the intermission was close to being over. There was the tingling. Before stopping to assess the situation, I suddenly forced myself up out of my chair and towards him. Upon getting there, I had no idea what to say. I self consciously muttered "can you give a blessing to an older girl?" He sharply asked "What did you say?" I had to repeat myself. "Why do you say that?" he asked accusingly. It scared me, but I continued, leaning in closer so he could hear. "Well, a little bit older.." I smiled a little. He mercifully let the issue go, and proceeded to bless me. My knees were shaking as he held his finger to my forehead. I realized I had been grasping his left hand tightly with my right for support. I said a heart-felt "thank you" and stepped quickly to the side and out of the way. As I turned back to look one last time at him before heading for my seat, I'll never forget the look on his face. His eyes had followed me with an astonished smile. I never was sure what that expression meant. But a great divide had been crossed. Thank you dear Yogananda. You prepared me for every step.

 Now, let me go back a moment. Within the story of that first trip to Ananda, there is also a curiosity I could share. It's really kind of interesting that there was a premonition attached to the preparation of this journey.

As I was describing, after Swamiji's suggestion that I visit Ananda, I was of course so excited to be actually going. I felt like Swamiji must have felt; wanting so badly to meet Yogananda. Yes I had decided. I could purchase a plane ticket. I can maneuver my way around a city airport and drive a rental car out into the country, and find this place.

I had some extra money to do it, which was in itself a very uncommon encouragement. Tax time had left me with some extra funds. But, it was also a bit of a harrowing prospect. I hadn't been on a plane in years, and had gotten complacent. There was a fire of new hope burning in me now though, at the thought of actually seeing him in person. So, I booked the flight. It happened that not long after, I had a dream I was on the plane, and it took a plunge. We were going down. I remember first thinking only "these people are scared. I have to help". Then I closed my eyes and fervently cried "Master!". As the plane continued to go down I tried to emote a calm aura, and somehow I completely and utterly put my life in his hands. The other thing that seemed to be in my mind, was a steady anticipation of my demise and making sure I pass this test. I was calming myself the whole time and preparing to jump upward to him when the time was just right.

I had done this kind of thing once, in a motorcycle accident when I was a teenager. I had been riding on the back and thinking that my friend Jeff wasn't very well in control. I felt something coming. So, I became very limber, and waited. When a car came around the bend too wide, and we hit the shoulder of the hi-way, I aimed outward to a level spot in the ditch and did a volley ball roll off my shoulder toward it, landing safely. This time, however I had an infinitely better place to land if I could only maneuver it perfectly; Master's arms. I was waiting at the spiritual eye. Suddenly, the dream ended, I thought, (it was kind of blurry) with us hitting the earth, and the beginning of a collision.

I woke up feeling warm and safe though. I was very pleased in fact, with myself for behaving the way I did in the crash dream. In the weeks to come, however, I started to wonder if my actual flight would be safe. When the time came, I decided it was silly to be superstitious. And, besides, Master had come when I called him. Also, if I were to die, I had found him in my life. So it would be okay to die I reasoned. So I did go.

I found it a bit eerie then, when at our second flight connection that day, we were informed while waiting to board, that we were being re routed to a different plane and boarding gate. As I was trying to catch up with the moving crowd, the pilot actually passed swiftly by me, and I had opportunity to quickly ask "What's the matter"? "They found a malfunction on our plane at the last minute." He said.

(Chorus)
Out of this love for you
there's a reason do do all that I can do
out of this love for you
will come a way to do whats right
when I make a new start
to get to where you are
destiny's out of my hands
straight out of my heart

there's a time in the morning with the first breath of day
the sun comes in you're there again to light up the way
there are tears in my eyes for the joy in my heart too great to be told
when the clouds disappear before my eyes so that I can soar

(Chorus)

you've always been beside me every step of the way
I just know—it's in my soul it's in the wind it's down the road
and i think of that load you held on your shoulder hour after hour
so i can stand before my God this day In your awesome power
(Chorus)

(song by michael shellard and sharon)

If Swamiji has, in meditation or during a quiet introspective moment, ever noticed someone's spirit soaring joyously very, very close to him, it could very well have been me listening to his music.

Maybe it was the song 'Love is the dawn of understanding', 'Love is a magician', 'Iomar6', or literally hundreds of other songs as beautiful as those. The song may be sweetly tinged with renaissance, or of a luring Celtic flavoring. It may be wafting me through a stoic medieval setting, or into the most wistfully enchanted scenery. Oftentimes it will be bittersweetly gypsy. But it will always irresistibly grip me.

Nothing in itself has done so much to change me in a fundamental way as the music this man has drawn from the spheres. It is literally out of this world. I know I have to say something about his music in this writing, although I am out on a limb here.

It is up to Master what I write, for I surrender this subject especially, to him. Music for me is something so deep, that I have no words.

So much of the wonderment indeed, is actually a deep contentment, born of the feeling that this music has always been the underscore of my very life's journey; that every adventure i have undertaken to inspiration --had one of his songs as a backdrop, whether it was in the playground of my beloved Camilla school, the church, or the mystic wanderings of my footsteps and daydreams through the fields and trails of my homeland. His music has somehow always been a part of my being

One day, while pondering the existence of Swami Kriyananda as a person, I remembered him thinking of his own guru; Master. How could Master be so deep in his heart, and yet be so unassumingly standing there on the other side of the room. This soul that he longed to melt into and be not only close to but one with, was also a man, seen by all. Within the moment of Swamiji's wonderment, Master walked up to him and smiling, handed him an apple.

I pass through the wee dawn hours of many nights deliriously happy as Swamiji's songs float through me. I repeat in a whisper "I love you sir" and, when worldly thoughts creep into my bliss, I say "neti neti" (not this, not that), open my spine again all the way up to the spiritual eye, and sink in.

Sometimes it almost seems as though he has been waiting for me, and is happy to settle into the warm nest I have prepared to adore him. If I should awaken partially, and one of his songs is not playing in my heart, then I choose one and put it in.

Here I was this one day then, as I was saying, listening to one of his cds at my desk. As the music was welling up inside me, I happened to glance over at his picture. That was one of those moments you treasure forever. I saw Swami Kriyananda. I mean, I really saw him. The outpouring of selfless love from the eyes was utterly staggering. Here was the love of God itself.. Lover, loved, loving; it was all of these.

Oh Swamiji, devotee knows how sweet you are. He knows who you let know. Engrossed is the bee of my mind, on the blue lotus feet of my divine mother.

  That instance has sustained me through many a trial. I am able to turn to you for unconditional love at my most vulnerable times. When I falter, and start to think of you as only a man, I call on this single experience that is forever embossed in my heart. You are my greatest comfort here on Earth.

MORNING SONG   GREETS THE DAWN

THERE YOU ARE   I'VE COME TO KNOW YOU

DON'T DEPART   HEARTH OF HEART

MINE THOU ART   YOU ARE WELCOME HERE

....

SO IT IS YOU CAME TO STAY   ONE DREARY WINTER'S DAY

A TEARDROP LET YOU IN   WITH THE WINDOW'S OPENING

A STREAM BEGAN TO FLOW   A LOVE FROM LONG AGO

THERIN BEGAN TO GROW   AS I HELD YOU NEAR

....

I AM AWAKENING   I HEAR YOUR BECONING

I'M LEARNING HOW TO SING WHILE THE WINTER TURNS TO SPRING

....

HOW FAR I FELL YOU KNOW   STILL YOU DID NOT LET GO

YOUR HAUNTING MELODY   FOUND A WAY TO FOLLOW ME

IT TRICKLED DOWN INSIDE THE WALL

WHERE LOVE HAD BEEN DENIED AND HOW

THE WITHERED ME INSIDE

HAS BLOSSOMED WITH THE DAWN

(song I wrote to Swamiji for his birthday)

Swami,
It's not easy to relate in words what your music does for me. I have tried in my writings.
It simply saves my life here in the world. Maybe the best way to describe it is
if I were your child say, and a catastrophe hit. You let go of my hand, and told me to wait for you.
You gave me the music box, and said "I'm in here, till I get back. I will be back to get you."
Then you disappeared into the crowd. Terrorized and frightened, I yet maintain my composure.
My beloved would never lie to me. He will come back for me.
And in the music I feel him, and his promise.

One time I was at our big gala "Canadian Country Music Week" in Winnepeg Manitoba. I was by then a recording artist, and had been asked to return there to host a writer's night at a lounge amidst the celebrations. There were many stars there. Among them was one of the aboriginal actors Tom Jackson.

My brother in law worked for Native Affairs out of Edmonton, and he had hoped that I might attract the support of some such high profile person as this to assist a program he was initiating to help the native kids who were struggling in the city. Upon seeing Tom, I made a b line toward him, thinking it best to just go ahead and approach him. If I second guessed, I might falter. Well, there I was in front of him. I had his attention alright. But, I couldn't get any words out. After about six or seven seconds of the most earnest stuttering, he burst out "Whatever it is, the answer is YES!"

I wanted so deeply for Swamiji to visit my dreams the way Master had been. I was so urgent in my longing, that finally, he did start showing up. It was like Master's first visits; rather distant and hazy, and I couldn't really get close to him.

Then I dreamed I was in some kind of Ashram. It was like a church, but in the city. I was led into a room to wait, and in walked Swamiji, dressed in rather royal looking attire. Just he and I were in the room, but I could sense there was a protocol to be adhered to. I sat quietly, and he sat on a stool right in front of me, facing me. He took out a guitar and sang me a song. I was enthralled. How many times I had been completely overwhelmed by his music. I listened courteously, and when it was over, I rose and made a nice respectable exit. However, once in the lobby, I realized I had lost my car keys. Not wanting to make a spectacle, I became nervous, and a few people were trying to assist me with some directions when who should enter the lobby to walk through, but Swamiji. He looked over at me, and kept going. I went outside where I continued my confusion privately. It was so much less than the impression I would have liked to have made. But, when I realized he had fully entered a dream and had attended to me, I was thrilled.

You were beckoned Sir, and you **did** come. Then Swamiji, you came to visit me again. More than that; you bent to press your cheek to my chest
and there you gave my heart its rest. I never will forget this kindness.

I have had the feeling of rising phoenix-like up through the murky swirls of meditation's beginnings, as if hanging by a thread and grasping finally, the new world. It dawned on me this morning what it is very much like. Anyone who has slalom skied (skied on only one ski) on water will know this. When you launch in shallow water, you can just hold the foot with the ski up, and when the boat takes off with the slack in your rope tightening, you can just step up onto the surface with your ski, level to the water and stand up. But what I'm talking about is if you have fallen in deep water, and you have to get back up on the ski from there; kind of like if you've fallen into some deep distractions in life, and you must

reach for Master from there. You put your bent leg out in front of you and aim your ski upward. Your free leg stretches out behind rather like a rudder. Try to relax. You are holding the rope, and when the boat takes off and your slack tightens, pulling you up swiftly, then is your moment. Your balance kicks in and you lift your core to be erect, holding it strongly from bottom to top. You start to flail and the waves are thrashing a great pressure all around you. You descend into the depths for that one moment where it's a dark, turbulent no-man's land. This is where many will fail. But, you surrender, close your eyes tight, and see yourself thrust upwards towards the first gleamings of the sun. And by God, you find yourself coming straight up out of the water, and finally astro-planing the surface. Someone watching from the boat will see a storm of swirling uncertainty, and a ski starting to steady itself. Then suddenly a head appears above the spray, and the body rises triumphantly. Then you are gliding smooth and effortlessly. You have progressed beyond the level of discontentment in your meditation by your incessant, unrelenting reaching for Master. When the confusion clears, you will find you have completed your ascension into a deeper level. You steadied your focus on the spiritual eye while plunging into the mystic, surrendering into the magnetic flow there, and finally emerging to find a new door opened.

THE MORNING SUN
SPREADS ACROSS THE LAWN
  AS I WAKE WITH THE MELODY
OF THIS SONG
  AND THERE'S NOT A SOUL HERE
TO SING IT TO
  MASTER COULD I SING TO YOU

FOR I HAVE BEEN LONELY AND I'VE BEEN SEARCHING
FOR SOME KIND OF LOVE I KNOW'S A SURE THING
  JUST LIKE THE FEELING OF BEING HOME
    IN MY FATHER'S HOUSE

OH WHAT I'D GIVE IF I COULD BE
  A MEMBER OF YOUR FAMILY
THEN THE ONE WHO MEANS SO MUCH TO ME
  COULD SEE HOW HARD I TRY

AND IT WOULDN'T MATTER IF I SHOULD FALL
  YOU'D HOLD ME TILL IT DIDN'T HURT AT ALL
AND THERE'D BE NO REASON TO EVER LEAVE ME
OUT HERE ON MY OWN

IF I COULD BE YOUR LITTLE GIRL
YOU'D NEVER BREAK MY HEART FOR SURE
YOU'D TAKE MY HAND   LEAD ME THROUGH YOUR WORLD
IF I WERE YOUR LITTLE GIRL

AND IT WOULDN'T MEAN I WAS A FOOL
TO WANT THE WHOLE WORLD TO KNOW THAT I LOVE YOU
AND IT WOULDN'T MEAN YOU WERE LEADING ME ON
TO HOLD ME IN YOUR ARMS

AND MAYBE SOMEDAY   I WOULD BE STRONGER
THEN I'D BE THE LIGHT YOU'RE DEPENDING ON TO
MAKE LIFE BETTER GROWING TOGETHER
  EVER BY YOUR SIDE

IF I COULD BE YOUR LITTLE GIRL
YOU'D NEVER   LET ME DOWN FOR SURE
YOU'D TAKE MY HAND   LEAD ME THROUGH YOUR WORLD
IF I WERE YOUR LITTLE GIRL

(song by sharon)

YOU'RE IN MY BLOOD LIKE HOLY WINE

YOU TASTE SO BITTER AND SO SWEET

OH I COULD DRINK A CASE OF YOU

AND STILL I'D BE ON MY FEET

I WOULD STILL BE ON MY FEET..   (Joni Mitchell)

I always remembered it being especially painful to me, the times when our dogs would, out of loving adoration for us, try to come along down the road. Especially the puppies. You had to scold them and chase them back, like you were mad at them. That's the only way they would end up turning back for home with their tails between their legs. That was where they were safe. That was where their center was they could maneuver from. To let them wander around was dangerous, and not a good way to train a dog to adhere to its path in life.

Well, I have written Swamiji a third song. It is beautiful I think. It seems to me Master was helping with the inspiration, just as he was in the first two I wrote for Swamiji. Oddly though, this is the only time Master didn't come to me in a dream afterward. I've just had my second contact with Swami Kriyananda a few months ago, at my second Spiritual Renewal Week at Ananda. Once again I waited until the Peace Treaty play, but I saw an occasion to approach him at the beginning, just before the play started.

As I've mentioned, he has responded to some of my letters throughout the years, and seemed to appreciate both the songs I had sent him. He also commented on an attempt I had made at writing prose; a story I exuberantly delved into; fantasizing I was a character in his recent Time Tunnel story. In an email response after receiving the song I had sent him, he had actually sent me a rough draft of the story. I was utterly thrilled.

Swamijii's love is so infectious, that it exudes out of all of his projects, making one feel a full part in the bliss of it all. As soon as I read the

Time Tunnel story about him and his little brother, I felt like I knew him better.

It was such a warm and captivating story, that I spontaneously wrote a chapter extending the story and adding myself as a character into the mix. It was so much fun, and I sent it to him.

But, I think I have been a bad little puppy. I have indulged too much in letting myself write letters to him, like he was a buddy of mine. It's hard though, to not seek that beautiful warmth one feels when his attention is on you..

I approached him right before the play, as I said. I knelt down and said "Swamiji, I am your friend Sharon". He was so gracious and took my hand, looking at me inquisitively. I stated further "I wrote you a song". "Which song" he asked. I began to get nervous. I looked down and uttered "The one for your birthday". "Oh, yes" he chimed. "I will write you another one for Christmas" I said eagerly. He smiled "okay". I looked happily into his eyes for a moment and let go of his hand. Then I went back to my seat.

Barely two months had gone by and I had written, recorded, and sent him his Christmas song already, in September. It had violins and a cello. I never heard from him about the song.* I keep reminding myself what a blessing that he ever took notice of me at all. Still, I am heartbroken. And I instinctively know these are the times spiritual progress has its best potential. You can never count on the person. It is the spirit of the ocean of consciousness we are all part of that is inherently ours. Not any one person within it. Swamiji would never compromise. He rather, fashions opportunities for growth where he can.

Just think of the old woman who gave Swamiji singing lessons when he was young. When she got attached; so much so that she was only living to see him become a great singer, he cut her off sharply. He never went back to her.

 In my meditation I am opening to take in the higher realms. Almost desperately I'm looking for any opening I can use to advance in a real

---

*at the time of this writing I hadn't yet heard from him about it.

way upward and outward. I'm glad Swamiji encouraged me with letters to give me a good start. But he knew when to stop.

By loosening the apron springs, I finally went on exploring some of the other aspects of God. Like, perceiving the sound of aum and the inner light, looking for bliss, feeling power developing. And, so very rewarding is the inkling that maybe I could be a channel for others thirsting as I do. So many need help so badly, and if I can do well, well then I could pitch in a hand. I want to help everybody, as Swamiji does. Just think when the seven cowboys of Silverado suddenly appeared over the crest of that hill, galloping to the rhythm of thundering hooves, with the sun beaming through the mountains behind them, and the big crescendo of music. The whole crowd in the movie theatre suddenly broke into cheering.

Those were all of one accord, and were returning to save the town. The turning point! A few mental citizens with fire in their hearts would be able to help the magnetism of the whole body to reach for the higher realms. Such is a sign that the worst of the battle was already over. I will stay on my path as best I can.

He wrote three words concerning my Time Tunnel side story effort that are indelibly printed in my mind. "I encourage it". And that is why I am writing this. It is all I have of his instruction to cling to right now. And, I want so to please him. If he is indeed revealing a duty of mine, I certainly don't want to miss it. I want rather, to be like the bridesmaid; waiting always, and ready with my lamp lit, and plenty of oil.

Master told Swamiji that he would grow on the path through writing about it. I suspect that is why I had that word of encouragement. And, it is amazing some of the insights and inspirations I am experiencing just writing this little book of mine. I am so thankful. It's funny too, that here I sensed Master's involvement very keenly. When the thought of writing a book seemed absurd, I saw his eyes urging me somehow. So, I stayed open and started thinking about what had happened. I replayed it in my mind;

Swamiji had actually sent me some advice on writing too, as a result of my sending that little story to him. Not only the statement about encouraging me in my writing, but instruction.

But, what I had written and sent to him was inspired by something I read that **he** had written. I kept thinking, Swamiji **encourages** it. And, in his letter back to me, he also had asked "Are there going to be any more sequels to my story?" But.. there's nothing that could be added to the story I had written to him. Or was there?

Well, the story that had inspired the little spin off of mine was his Time Tunnel children's story. I couldn't continue to write about that. It was his idea and not mine. So I wrote him another song. I had uttered to him at our meeting that I would write him a song for Christmas and I had to follow through on that. **But, it hadn't endeared me to him. And, Master's eyes weren't satisfied. He wasn't letting me off the hook.** Then it occurred to me that I could include my sequel to his story in a story about my insights in meditation within the larger framework of my life experiences; a story in a memoirs format, if you will. **This** story! Could it be that this is what he wants me to write? He seems much more contented now when I look at his picture.

So at this time let me introduce an interlude section herewith, about a little boy named Donnie Walters, who had found a time tunnel with his brother, and his finding of a new friend:

In the spring of the next year, Donny's mother was able to bring them early for holiday season to the inn. She loved to help Frau Weidi find the best fresh produce for the meals. It gave her wonderful missions to go on, and she started visiting a poor Gypsy woman in a valley not but about 8 miles away. The lady sold eggs and mother went out of her way for these eggs, and began to visit for hours in the beautiful spring mornings when she was in an especially inspired mood. The drive was especially pretty too, and the cottage although simple, was rustic and so cozy looking.

Donny there met Rose. That first day he waited for mother to leave, as he was expecting them to continue on, making a trip to the farmer's market in nearby Tecuci. But, lingering along the back yard fence, he noticed the beautiful rolling hills and meadows on the other side. The lady's daughter; Rose appeared.

Right away he saw that her bright dark eyes could see right into you. She was very quiet, but Donny was somehow drawn to her. They sat quietly in that morning sun under a tree. Finally mother came, and Donny was reluctant to leave even though they hadn't spoken a word to each other.

A couple of weeks later, Mother again went for eggs, although there were still a dozen and a half in the fridge. Donny wanted to go too. He asked Rose if she would show him where the path in the pasture led to. She happily took his hand and began through the gate. This was the beginning of a strange, new and beautiful friendship. For, as much as Donny usually evaluated things, Rose dismissed them. She said that only fools and grocers weigh things. Rose said it seemed that all that was stretched out at the end of her outreached hand probably disappeared when she looked the other way. And that a new world then appeared *there* for her to experience. Rose didn't have any toys to play with. But one day she and Donnie sat on a hillside and played a kite game. After the quietness got close up and warm feeling, at her instruction, they started to breath upward with open mouths together.

They had to make a special little effort to get that breath back a bit into the spine where the liveliness of the breath would be sucked up naturally, like in an air vent. That wasn't too hard. It only took the energy to want to keep up with Rose. Then, at the bottom of the spine, they formed a kite in their minds and put their heart in it so it could feel where it was going. A little glimpse of the room at the very bottom near their tailbones, and they were off. They touched on the next room gliding up. It was a few inches up. Then the next was near their belly buttons. The next, where the kite started to feel at home, and really free..was behind their hearts. Then to the throat, behind their eyes, and finally out the top of their heads. By this time there was a tingling freeness and the kite was happy. It floated up there for a time, and then folded, becoming a streamlined arrow, and glided slowly straight back down through all the rooms with their relieved exhaling breaths.

At first it was kind of a journey, and Donnie stayed there with Rose. But after a time he melted into her and the kites became just a pretty light on its way to the top opening, and then looping back around gaining momentum and becoming lighter and prettier and freer with every rotation.

The rooms too began to take on characteristics of their own. The bottom ones were strong and solid and the upper rooms were breezy and magical. Rose said that the kite was used to living at the bottom usually. It was a good place to start a kite's journey. But because it was a kite, it was meant for finding a way to the top rooms where it could do what it was meant to do. She said because the kite had become so used to the bottom, that some work had to be done to let it know it was free to move up. This game was good. But, she had another game too. In order to move up, the kite had to want to let go of what was under it. So much habit and attraction to the humdrum of the lower rooms had accumulated, that they would have to visit those rooms one by one to clean them out and say goodbye. It would take some time. But it was a fun game. And through the learning and planning, Rose's spirit was becoming more and more beautiful to Donny. She was a true friend and somehow he wanted to go where she would be..

He slowly started to realize too that the kite was he, and that there was somewhere he needed to be that wasn't related to time at all --or places, for that matter. It wasn't even related to his world or his body, really. For they were connected with the bottom rooms.

Donnie thought of how he had melted into Rose, and he realized in a glimpse, that God had led him to her. And deeply under all of this, there was God smiling. He had never known him so sure before. But then, he had never put forward his full effort in love before. If Rose cared for him, how much more God must, to show himself this way, and show him this pathway. How else would he have found out about the upper rooms? He knew deep within him somehow, too, that someday he would have to give up Rose. She would melt into God for good. Even his own self would. And that will be the most joyful thing he could feel, even though his current feelings would have to be tamed to make this leap. Maybe this next game would help with this too. Suddenly he realized he wanted to go home. His real home-- that he somehow had gotten so far away from. In this moment, He wanted it so much, that he knew he could now not settle for anything less. On to the next game then..

As they sat in the tall swaying grass on their next visit, Rose told Donnie that they would need help with this new game.

"There are Masters" she said, "who want us to find God. They were here in the world like us at one time. They too endured many lifetimes before they became enlightened and found God. They too learned how to go inside and find the higher realms. They want very much to help us now, as we are all part of God". She touched her heart, and looking up, said these beautiful words;" thou hast made us for thyself and we are restless until we find our rest in thee".

If all of us together are as an ocean, then we can be truly at peace with him when the water is waveless and still. You and I can't be part of that blissful expanse when we are restless.

Donnie asked "Who are these Masters that will help us with our next game"? They are Yogananda, Sri Yukteswar, Lahiri Mahasa, Babaji Krishna, Jesus himself, and a teacher named Swami Kriyananda. Donnie was excited. He chose this as the time to tell her about his time travelling. "I will find out about them" he said, "so that I can truly tune into their help and appreciate where they have come from and why". Rose shyly smiled. "I have been time travelling too" she said. And that was all she said.

Donnie, upon returning home later, started to travel to the times of these Great men. They were from India, except for Jesus .Swami Kriyananda he didn't find. However, he observed the outward lives of the others. He admired each of them very much, and by the time he and Rose met again, he had learned a great deal. "Yogananda is alive now" he told her. I didn't find the Swami. Did he go by some other name? "Possibly", she smiled. "Never mind. That name shows up later in the future. That's why you didn't find it. You didn't look there. It's alright. You will learn about him now. He starts the game with us."

They sat and fell into the silence. Rose then whispered to go to the bottom room. It was at the base of the spine. First they had to tense the muscles there to tweak their concentration and hone in to the center of that area. It was kind of like pressing to a sizzling feeling, with the will to do something *now*, like you would do if you were rubbing 2 sticks together with the confidence that you can start a spark.

Then Rose gently, lovingly spoke "Swamiji where are you"..she then blissfully smiled. Swami's light entered softly. We must focus, said Rose. Swami's force became as a hand gently pulling their chins straight ahead to make strong eye contact. Look here.

They looked up into that light while swirling in the room. He then said "absorb this love. It is for you. Drink it in. Don't look away. Just bring it as close as you can and drink." The light vibrated with the energy that poured from it into the bottom room. A sort of tunnel developed which drew the grayness from that room and directed it upward and out.

They stayed fixed at that spot for a long time. They felt light headed, as if a load had been lifted. Rose said, "This is the Earth room. It corresponds to the inertia of our existence. The good solid foundation we need for a time, but the fixed preoccupation with forms and matter we don't. We have just gotten rid of a good amount of desires for that kind of thing, and old habits of leaning on the outward things of this world. Not just from this lifetime but others too. Swami says even a little desire for ice-cream was in those whirlpools that we are going to pull apart in time, with the vacuum of love, and release. Some day it will be clean in here. Then there will be no need for this room at all. For now though, let's move up to the next Chakra. For that's what these rooms are. Places where energy gets stopped along the astral spine, where the physical spine makes detours to serve our outer senses and extremities."

Who serves in the next place? Donnie asked. Swami Kriyananda again. Why does he help in the bottom rooms? There's no other like him, said Rose. He is the best at it. He has dedicated himself down in the trenches of this world, where the people need him the most. We are in an age where we can imagine God, but entrenched in the customs of the darker age that we came out of. We are painfully aware of our separation from God at this point, and there is great suffering in the knowing. But, there is no low place one can sink that Swami Kriyananda will not go in after you . He was commissioned by God to help us at this time. If nobody could get down here and get this energy moving in the first place, there would be no hope at all. He is not afraid, and he is 'The Communicator'. Supremely Intelligent, and intuitive too. His books, music, lectures and outreach communities have reached hundreds of thousands with real answers. He can figure out how to relate to anybody. He speaks the language of everybody. And so lovingly. He is the right hand man of Yogananda.

Donny really admired these qualities. He shone with affection for the Swamiji. Then he interjected, "Rose, you have been speaking strongly". Rose quietly said "I told you I had time travelled too.

What I didn't tell you was, I am from the future." "You are not the Gypsy woman's daughter"? "No, I came for you.."

"You can't do anything to *change* the future..can you"?

" You can change it with love", she said softly. "You won't outwardly remember any of this though..

Someday when you learn these things, they will not be as games. You will take to them easily, like you have craved for them. In fact you have, and have done them in many lifetimes. This lifetime is kind of important though, on a count of you are able to help so many people through your freedom in this one. It is your time.

Now", she said. " Back to the Chakras. Swami will help us again with the second one." They went from the first and crept up as if in a beam of upward sweeping fragrance, to a second room. This was the room of liquid..not so much a solid feeling place anymore, but a little more flowing. you could almost hear a flute calling. Swami's voice wafted in and out in a heartfelt song of longing to his father "Lord most high, our heavenly father, all our lives we dedicate to thee". The room became as a vast expanse of water, and his spirit settled at a distance within it. His soft light became slightly condensed and love vibrated out of it. "Come here" he softly murmured in a rich deep voice, and a thrust welled up inside them as to glide right over the water or any obstacle that was between they and he. They held him close, closer and closer, pulling his love into the room. He gave overflowingly, and they received all they could, absorbing this beautiful essence through the opening into the lower abdomen. Stay connected..catch all that is pouring out of this cup. They stayed connected, intensely at first. Then as the power poured more surely and evenly, they relaxed and felt the filling with great joy. So many urges and intentions would be alleviated through this channel in time. Urges that came from the bottom room and through here, that were associated with feelings people had in darker ages, and feelings that were of an animal instinct type. Even now it was started. And, what a relief.

"Thank you Dear Swami Kriyananda. Be not far away Father. " For this was the chakra of the guru, and their love was not misplaced in its gravity towards him.

He helped them upward with their fresh flow's release, and they found themselves on their way to the third room. This was the room of the Great Yogananda. It was fiery self control. There were swirls of pure power, arranged across a field along the waistline in even minded anticipation for a beckon call. This was the Chakra he had been in charge of in previous lifetimes, as the immemorial Arjuna in the battle of Kurukshetra, and as the mighty 'William the Conqueror'. In the first battle he courageously took on the opposing citizens of his own lower nature in an all out battle for the soul, on behalf of all humanity. In the second, he secured a beachhead for the east to merge with the west, making way for the coming teachings to take root and thrive.

This was not only the place where east met west, but where the lower rooms would converge into the higher. The mystic 'leap of faith' as it were. Donny suddenly saw the essence of this great master, and a warm thrill engulfed him as he recognized this force to be the very God figure he had perceived. There was no going back. They lingered here and pressed slowly more and more surely into this 'horizon of hope' into the unknown. The master's expansive 'ground of being' emerged slowly into them, adding the stability they needed to stay put. The power invited them, and finally accepted their willingness into the swell. The forces began to replenish their supplies.

Yogananda's eyes flowed with a love never imagined. They had pleased him in their intent to find him. They were ready to move farther up. Somehow they knew he would be here each time they ventured through, giving them a mission they could carry out, and not more. Surely and steadily they would develop the power to become Generals for him in this fight for true love; this quest for truth.

By the way, she said, "the purpose of all of this is to find bliss. It is the nature of joy to perpetuate itself. That's how we all got here; we are bliss projected out of the very consciousness of bliss that is God. And bliss is the trail back home. And, you must give your bliss back to God. That is what really feels good. But don't even do it to feel good. Do it for God. Action without desire for the fruits of action is the highest calling. Find bliss in the stillness within; in the essence that is God. We are all one in bliss; in love. On to the heart chakra. Sri Yukteswar of the heart.

Donny interjected "he was a little hard wasn't he" Rose said, "I had an uncle who used to scold. He was scary. But, I respected him so much and learned exactly what he intended.

Now I look back on him as maybe being the most loving of all my uncles. When I got older, I witnessed him winking in the middle of a scolding. Somehow I knew all along.

The most tender moment in all that I consider faith and scripture, was the moment Yogananda met this Master-- Sri Yuketeswar; his guru. It was in a most beautiful frailty that Yuketeswargy displayed his overwhelming love for the boy Mukunda; this precious student, this catalyst that would immerse the world into the timeless poetry of true love. Yes, this too was Yogananda. But Yukteswar had to carefully encourage a mixture of the warrior and the prince with extreme discipline and focus.

He is the kindest of souls. I will show you. They started to drift upward into the heart area. With some tension the area began to burst its boundaries and the Great Spirit began to enter. They knew how to hold this force blissfully then. There was nothing to do for the great father but enter and enjoy the fruit of all that labor of lifetimes. He blissfully dwelled in the Ganges river of eternity, and those who had come this far were his true children. He loved them as he had loved Yogananda, and the glory of the spheres was his mantle. His candle shone with all the colors of promise.

They fell at his feet in reverence. Lifetimes of worry and fear began to lift. His face began shedding layers of expression until it was finally the light of the heart itself. Nothing mattered. Oh, how beautiful it was to be here. They stayed for a long time. Then this airy love began to lift them again, like balloons. There was enough room in them for all humanity. They began to feel like kites again.

When you feel satisfied like we do here, Rose said, use this place then as a cliff to freefall bravely into the unknown ahead. Longer, deeper, farther we must go. The bliss began to get more intense. Lahiri Mahasaya awaited them, and this was the territory of the ego, at the medulla near the throat, where life begins on all levels of conception. This is where they not only had to slide past the ego, but to win it over into their upward stream. Like the subconscious, the ego had been a necessity in evolution. It let you know you were no longer in an animal mentality, and through it you developed the ability to perceive that you are one with God.

However, it kinda got stuck at the stage where first it realized you were a separate entity; to the extent that you could think different thoughts from others. That made it feel important, and lifetimes were spent spiraling off of your true path experimenting with painful experiences, always thinking they would lead somehow to happiness. If you only knew you didn't have to use this instrument of the ego. You only have to realize your true oneness with all that is.

But the ego had the monopoly on reason, letting you think you could figure out the path through it instead of bypassing it completely and using the intuition of the great "I AM". God could give you all you needed. The ego couldn't. It needed to be put in its subservient place of practical thinking on certain lower plains..just as the subconscious was given the task of being the workers on the lower floors of your factory; remembering processes, storing files, etc. These upper rooms were like the executive suites where everything ran smoothly, but you had to tame this Lion at the Gate, of the ego- into a pussycat who would lay down with the lamb.

Lahiri would help them in this room of ether. He had been the guru of Sri Yuketeswar. **In a former incarnation he had also been the radiantly mystic Muslim Sufi poet 'Kabir'.** His devotees could go into his ashram, and if they could fall very still they could see his beautiful spirit flickering. With love, they could get his attention and his twinkling eyes would shine ever so slightly in their direction. Lahiri valued your love so very dearly. He would do anything for you. He once materialized in a wheat field to coax the boss of a devotee to let the man make a pilgrimage to visit him. The man yearned so deeply to see his guru.

Lahiri had grown up in fairly material surroundings, had married and had children, with an accountant job. He knew the great divide that must be crossed by those who longed to reach God. Coming from a limiting background like this can sometimes fan the flames even more, and make your love all the more urgent. It's a harder reach, and Lahiri was even observed in mid air consumed in a roaring fire, so great was his offering to God.

Oh Lahiri, whispered Rose "I want so to please you in all things". They felt a cool breeze blowing through willow trees.

Once more they were in the pasture behind the Gypsy woman's house. It was the feeling Donnie had many times when he knew his mother would be wanting to go home soon, but he and Rose were so enthralled, that the sun was dancing upon the blades of grass, and a soft 'om' sound was swelling all around them, in and out of the slivers of light.

All the feelings of ecstasy they had ever known were all rolling up into one, and they put an invisible finger on it to keep it there. Pressing lightly, the ecstasy pulsed slightly, growing more and more delicious to the touch. They were careful as with an exquisite butterfly cupped in the palm, not to lose this captured rapture. They carefully placed it into the stream and began to move higher with it.

Babaji! the name was musical and beautiful. "He's not far away" whispered Rose. They were at the spiritual eye. This was where the stream ended. You could reach God from here. They tightened their eyes shut with such a devoted willingness to see Babaji. He was right behind the eyes, in the middle of the forehead.

As Krishna, he had driven Arjuna's chariot, winning him the final victory over the senses, when the ego itself had finally been persuaded to give up the fight. It was he who revealed to Arjuna the wondrous joy that indeed, nothing had died. All the fallen soldiers of bad habits and desires had only been transformed into the finest of qualities. The forces that held to them all those eons of time were actually neutral. When Arjuna and Krishna won them, they used those forces to populate more instances of the goodness that was in *them*; Kindness, generosity, love, patience. A most incredible victory it was. This was the way God had intended these forces to be used.

And indeed that's really what was going on now. The children were slowly replacing the bad tendencies within them with good ones, freeing up the energy that held those bad tendencies- that had been clogging up the chakras, in whirlpools of knots and hardness, waiting for the right karmic time to be unleashed. They had been stored there, but they didn't actually need to be used. Replacing all those expectancies with no expectation at all, made room for virtue to happily, simply and quietly reside there. These games were good practice for developing this proper use of power.

And Babaji was not in the war as Krishna now. He was assisting to achieve these virtues playfully and happily. He resided in an enchanted cave in the Himalayas, and children such as Donny and Rose could happen upon it playing innocently in the forest. If they loved deeply, they could see him. He was ever so beautiful with long copper flowing hair and a chiseled angelic face emoting the deepest reverence.

Babaji had been approached by Jesus. He helped put together the techniques of the games, and the plan to train Yogananda, because this kind of help was again needed. The world was crying for it. Especially in the west where they had become very practical and intellectual, but were realizing something essential was missing. Jesus had many followers in the west but few of them were looking for him and experiencing him intimately like this, where they could really glean from him.

Jesus had come in a dark age, and the deeper subtleties' of his teachings had been misunderstood. The timeless ancient teachings of the East in India could be very beneficial at this stage. The beautiful fact was, Babaji, Lahiri, and Sri Yukteswar had stayed close to this son of God. They had been the wise men who noticed him being born and followed his star. And, although Donnie found Jesus being the one not from India, in fact he went there to find his friends again when he was a teenager. The bible writings lost track of him during this time. But it was documented in the east.

*

He is the only begotten son of the father; not his body of course. But, the only way one can be the 'begotten'; the only way God can fully dwell in one was to attain the consciousness Jesus had attained. The reflection of God in him was spotless. He had overcome and could sit at the right hand of the father. His message was that the kingdom of God is within you, and you too can "overcome and sit at the right hand of God" and "go out no

---

* The only way you **can** *be saved indeed, is through Christ. This is not the last name of Jesus. Christ means "anointed one". It is the root meaning of Krishna too. To become anointed is to become chosen. It takes a lot of hard work on your part too, to become God's chosen.*

more" into this progression of lifetimes. You can finally be "heir to the kingdom" and brother to Jesus. Do not your scriptures say ye are Gods? He had said. Krishna's name too means 'anointed one', like "Christ". The Masters were free as Jesus is. This is the most magnificent help mission one could imagine!

Babaji's advanced student was Lahiri. Donny began to realize the kind of potential that was being offered to humanity at this time. The magnetism developing at the spiritual eye was palpable. There were great forces at work here. It was like an opening into the sky.

"Make straight the way of the lord", Donny beamed, remembering, as the energy came gushing upward swiftly from the very bottom of the spine to the spiritual eye and then started funneling upward. "Heaven and earth is filled with his Glory. When thine eye is single thy whole body be full of light. Come unto me little children. For of such is the kingdom of God." The words of Jesus kept flowing floodlike, out of the beautiful Om vibration all around them.

Heaven opened up above them and they lingered there in ecstasy. Donny didn't really know how long they were there. There were no questions. All there was in this region were answers that dissolved into love. Finally Rose whispered "Go on alone.."

Donny opened his eyes and looked at her. "Alone..Rose"? She blissfully looked at him and said "That is what my great teacher has taught me. It will be the final step to liberation. And, the time has come for me to leave you. . Soon." Donnie reflected for a moment.

"Is Swami's name Donnie"?

Rose just smiled.

"He taught me everything I know. He has been such a warrior for God, that he hasn't even had a family. He was totally dedicated to his guru. It must have broken his heart when Yogananda died after just three and a half years. Swamiji was so young.

So many people love him. He is the object of everyone's affection. And mine. However, he must be totally free when he kicks his body someday. His Guru said he will be.

I know that he must have one perfect relationship in this life to achieve this. It is not only a requirement, but something he so deserves. Maybe he has fulfilled the requirement many times over. I simply don't know. However, knowing how he is; neglecting himself in service to others, he may not have manifested it for himself.

I came back here to make sure. Insurance, as it were. His guru left him so young, and of his followers , there may be a perfect love". Then her voice quivered. "But I wanted to love him perfectly too, in this beautiful time and place. Not just to make sure he makes it—not that.. but, because.. I just had to.

I didn't find the time tunnel the way you did. I got here by sheer longing. I.. just wanted to know him" she sighed. Donnie looked at her deeply. Then, true to his tender nature, a tear formed in his eye.

But I can assure you my dear reader, that that sacred tear was never allowed to touch the ground.

THE END

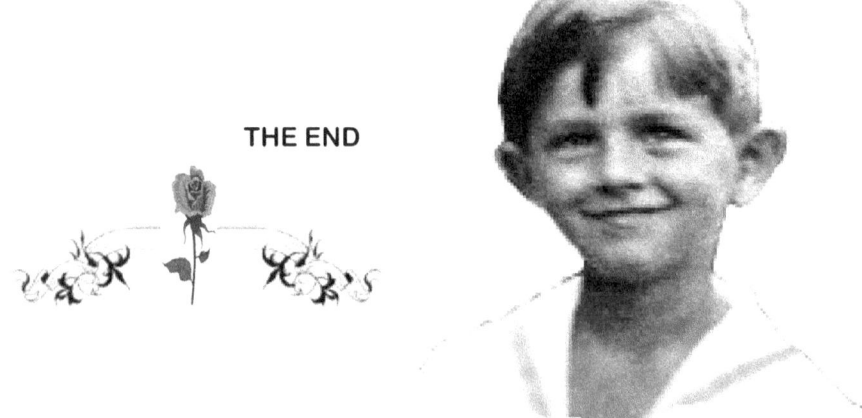

BRIGHT EYES WITH ROSY CHEEKS   HOW COULD ANY CHILD SMILE SO SWEET

EVEN THE WIND WANTS TO FOLLOW YA   LITTLE PIED PIPER OF ROMANIA

SING YOUR SONG DONNIE   SPEAK OUT LOUD

BUILD YOUR RAINBOW THROUGH THE CLOUDS

YOU ARE HERE BY GODS OWN HAND

SAINT JAMES   DONALD WALTERS   KRIYANANDA

THE DISCIPLINE OF MORAL LAW   YOU BROUGHT TO AMERICA

AND MET THE SPIRAL OF A DOWNWARD PULL WITH THE POWER OF YOUR WILL

I WAS HERE WHEN IT ALL CAME DOWN   THIS FEELS LIKE HALLOWED GROUND

SHOULDER TO SHOULDER AND SIDE BY SIDE   OUR SOULS LIVE HERE UNIFIED

YOU CAME ON THE WINGS OF TRUTH   SERVING AS YOUR GURUS PROOF

AND HIS GREAT SALVATION PLAN

SAINT JAMES   DONALD WALTERS   KRIYANANDA

IN THE BOOK OF HISTORY   A MAN CAME IN A TIME OF NEED

BUT IN THE ESSENCE OF ALL THAT'S TRUE

IT'S JUST SO GOOD TO BE LOVED BY YOU

YOU DIDN'T HAVE TO COME BACK AT ALL

BUT YOU JUMPED DOWN OFF THAT WALL

LEAD US ON TO   THE PROMISED LAND

SAINT JAMES   DONALD WALTERS   KRIYANANDA

(Kriyananda by Sharon)

Master said that a man who is thirsty and wants to drink the whole lake, finds he can only drink three cups of water. So we would like to love so deeply, but haven't the capacity yet. That's what we are working towards. But I think we know what it will be like when we start making headway. I was distracted with outward things in my meditation today, and visiting each chakra, I couldn't get the baby to focus her attention on each area. Finally at the spiritual eye, something caught her attention, and she gleefully giggled. Then we were there. All the focus of her whole world was on her one treasure. Just like when Emily was a baby and we would play "this little piggy went to market", or Winka Market, as she called it. When it came to the Weee Weee Weee, all the way home part, she drank the whole ocean. When Nathan first saw Toy Story, he was a toddler. After the movie, I heard his little voice joyfully singing "you Gotsa friend in me". He was drinking the whole ocean. We once saw a Harry Potter movie at the theatre. Afterwards in a toy store I passed an aisle and witnessed him trying to draw a toy sword off the floor with his concentration. He had drunk the whole ocean. Be thou a yogi.

I used to wander the fields from Calahoo, behind Labonte's and out towards Snooky's corner and the farm. I loved the rolling hills and sweet smelling waving wheat. At the bottom of the big hill, was a homestead place nestled into a meadow there along a tree line; a very pleasant dwelling. For some reason people didn't ever live there for long. It was abandoned much of my childhood. Mitchells finally moved their big family of playful children in there. But this was long before that. I saw it at the bottom of the hill this day, and ambled towards it, coming in from the back. I was maybe 6 or 7. It was a quiet day, serenely so, and I was entranced by natures beauty and the trickling trills of nearby birds gathering into little symphony swells.

Then a fragrance found me, and as I entered through the back gate of the yard, I saw what I thought at first was a dream; a myriad of flower gardens. Grand, huge bowing colored flowers mingled with frail flowing wild flowers. The soil had been lovingly tended into a rich black foundation of mounds, yielding patchworks of elegance and cultivated to perfection. Everywhere there were all varieties of flowers; even the kinds that Mrs. Kolesar took so much pride in displaying at her entrance. Around every corner of the house this garden reached out blissfully, flourishing with greater and greater beauty.

"Who made such a garden?" I wondered, as I ventured up onto the doorstep and in through the creaky old door of a house that had no sign of people having been there for years.

I spent the better part of the day playing there, sinking deeper and deeper into the magical world within; a world that had manifested when my thoughts had themselves been a very garden of love. I never saw it there again, but even now I can go there. Master, you love me so. Please don't ever stop calling me home..

LOVE IS A ROSE

BUT YOU BETTER NOT PICK IT

ONLY GROWS WHEN IT'S ON THE VINE

HAND FULL OF THORNS AND YOU KNOW YOU'VE MISSED IT

LOSE YOUR LOVE

WHEN YOU SAY THE WORD 'MINE' (from a neil young song)

Swamiji says we are all one. And, that being nice to someone is being good to your expanded self. Being jealous or mean is doing that to your own self and defeats expansion. Could it be that the first and most cherished perception from infancy really is true; All is love?

I was editing a book yesterday and came across a picture of a baby being born. The doctor and nurse were distracted, remarking something to each other, unaware of the heroic expression on the face of this entering pilgrim reaching skyward with an urgency of utter grasping hope. Had he come this far if it hadn't been inborn in him that he could do this? After all, he was God. This was no birth, just a ripple on the calm smooth expanse of infinity. Surely he could ride out this little ripple that was melting back into himself. But, inevitably he **would** start to drift out into this new world. If he knew how far out he could drift and how stranded he could become, well, perhaps like me he did know. But he had been so very close to the bosom for a time to have to be torn out in this cruel fashion. Yet there it was..the indelible hope in this little face shining out from underneath all the turmoil.

What a brave little soul.
Yes, I too am him as my heart
yearns for this world to be kind to him.
He really has no choice.

Like the snake in the Hindu rituals being lured up a tube. They say that's like the search for God, and then too, like the journey of this little soul all alone reaching up from the middle of nowhere. Stopping halfway is suicide. There's no way up or down. You have to surrender with desperate resolve that the current will carry you up with your own push.

If I can become free enough in meditation that my consciousness soars up high, then I have access to where Swamiji is. And his love is there for all, including me.

I have been emoting so penetratingly to him for so long now, in my obedience to developing devotion on my path. Finally It seems he has come to know me. If my awareness is in the lower chakras, I try to bring it up to the heart, and there it is much more like a child's love. His essence is so completely and unconditionally loving that it seems like he welcomes me with open arms. I become the channel for his bliss as I relinquish all that I am and all that I have into sparkling streams of upward adornment. He seems even to be happy I am here. Oh, this visit is so precious.

Yet, I know others are offering their bliss too. Many of them have been with him much longer. Is their joy mingled with mine, or much more dear to him, I start to delusively wonder. No! No, I too am they. And through the mist I am able to see a bridge all of them have made for me. I wander across it, up into the top; the area where there are no questions but just answers. And I am swirling with them. Their beautiful energy tingles within mine, and we all gather around our beloved Swamiji in a soft flickering of contented love. He swells to contain all with a twinkling smile.

Working slowly each kriya session to develop the inner strength to hold the chakras and channel open, and directing the flow of energy pointedly up into it, seems to me, like a dancer lifting the beautiful ballerina up into her elegant receiving position, and being able to hold her there so she can soar. Then, when she touches the sun, the rays filter down into you and you are part of her bliss.

angel   inner child   always knows   where I hide
within the tear   there is a gentle soul
where dreams unfold   and open wide

if you could only take to the sky   angel
you could surround anyone   who sees you as you are
rain down   angel
fall upon   the eyes of he   who sees the naked   beauty
and wash the rest away

angel I'm afraid   when passions rise   building up inside
your simple touch   becomes the way I feel
truths that reveal   rush in like the tide

if you could only take to the sky   angel
you could surround anyone   who sees you as you are
rain down   angel
fall upon   the eyes of he   who sees the naked   beauty
and wash the rest away

you are the seed that carries my spirit through the wind
you must reach the end   and don't give in
you paint beautiful pictures in my mind
angel   don't let them die
heaven's child   teach me to fly

(song by Sharon)

One of Swamiji's formost desiples; Asha Praver was confused in the early years of Ananda, and came to Swamiji for advice. As always he knew intuitively and instantly.
"It's so hard to know what God wants".
"No it's not".
That is all he said, but as I meditated later, I felt his conciousness say
"you don't really want to know what God wants" "You are afraid to know".
I realized I was avoiding what I was afraid of by pretending I was confused.
Later,
"Sir, whenever I'm confused about Gods will, it's that my fear is blocking my intuition?"
"Yes."
"So if I'm not afraid, then I'll be able to understand.."
"Yes". "It's not hard to know what God wants" He said again.
I changed my prayer from 'What does God want', to 'What am I afraid of'.
That desire for the truth is what gives us clarity of mind.
I reflected;
'How can Swamiji be so insightful. He can always find an answer.'
And I began to realize that the intelligence of his mind came from the courage of his heart. Because his heart is entirely committed to the simple truth.

He had a characteristic posture in that essentially he would meet life **Heart** first.
What did this 'posture' look like. Answer on next page

Spiritual development through yoga is not a system or a path; it's a definition—a description of what takes place as the soul evolves back toward a recognition of its own true nature. This is a reality that embraces the entire human race And whether you're Jewish or Catholic or Hindu or Buddhist or Muslim, you will have to follow this path because you were made in a certain way and there are certain realities that you are a manifestation of.

There is only one truth in the universe. Now I'm not saying therefore everybody has to take up yoga; everybody has to join this way or that way. I'm saying exactly the opposite of that. I'm saying that whatever teaching you might be followin if you're going in the right way these things will happen to you. The same truth is present at every level of manifestation. In his Raja yoga series, Swamiji speaks of your development of consciousness as being varying developments of a wave's closeness to its ocean body reality; near the top you are as the crest trying to break free of it while identifying only with your little self. In the middle you are a little closer to the surface, not thrusting out so greatly, and near the source as the base of the wave, you are saintly and clinging more to the vastness of ocean that is yours. Merging with the ocean is divine peace. Reality is directional, and like a magnet. Everything has a north and south pole. At the north pole of anything there is the south pole polarity, and at the south pole there is the corresponding north polarity. And, in nature when you are happy your energy naturally goes up in your spine. If you are headed constantly towards the north pole, you are doing all that is needed. Master's definition of self realization is the knowing in all parts of body, mind and soul that you are now in possession of the kingdom of God, that you do not need to pray that it come to you, and, that God's omnipresence is your omnipresence and all you need to do is improve your knowing. What we have to understand is that we have and are everything that we'll ever be right now. Everything is sweet and it all comes from feeling this inner consciousness of joy. The more you have of that, the more you don't need anything more. You can't be attached to things and meditate well. He goes on to say how you are naturally happy, until you see something you want; a car maybe. Then you place a limitation on the happiness, saying that it depends now on obtaining that car. The habit of nurturing thoughts of things that you want, multiplies-- thus the initial happiness become more and more buried. The reason people don't have peace is not that they haven't yet filled their desires, it's that they have desires in the first place. When you overcome desires you are effectively plugging the holes in your bucket. Always remember your joy is inside not outside. Yogis enjoy everything much more intensely. Desire is the only real enemy of human happiness. The less you want the more you'll have. Saint John of the Bible said if you want to be everything then desire to be nothing. Saints feel themselves not to be this body. There is great joy in being free that way. There comes a stage in meditation where your body will stop breathing for long periods of time. This kind of activity is a far more demanding kind of labor than working in an office and also far more productive. When you leave your body you can do a great many things that you can't do with the body. In 1961 director of the Zoological institute in Darjeeling spoke of a scientific expedition in the higher Himalayas where they came across a meditating Yogi above the tree line in lotus pose, in the stage of Samadhi. His fingernails had grown into the bark of the tree he was sitting under. They estimated he had been in this position for about six months. You might think he may as well be dead. In fact he is dead. But he is very much alive in another world. All the good that can come into the world comes from attunement with the infinite. The more we can act as windows for that infinite consciousness, the more we will be able to radiate waves of bliss into the world. Actively calm and calmly active, we should strive to be. Make work meditation, and meditation work.

THOU ART THAT

When Master had a school for young boys in the early days in India, they found a baby deer, and tenderly cared for it. It became a pet, and was exposed to an exalted level of awareness and affection. When it became sick Master prayed fervently. Finally the little deer manifested a deep ethereal pleading to the Master; "let me go". Master realized that he was impeding the spiritual evolutional path of the little animal. He knew they had to un-attach themselves and let it go..

Some years ago a stray cat donned our doorstep. We took her in and she had a litter of kittens in our den. Then she left. One of the kittens had long pure white fur and I named him Igloo. He was my heart's delight. But, because of his beauty, the neighbors also liked him, and he started crossing the dangerous road past our yard. The other cats seemed to be content to stay in the yard. When Igloo was killed it tore at me so that I could barely stand it.

Our daughter wanted a pet. I thought a bird would be nice to have, so we got a parakeet; Soto. It wasn't long before I grieved for him not having a bird friend of his own, and we got a female for him; Mrs. Wiggins. Then we found some u shaped tin pieces ideal for setting high up at the tops of the five windows in the den, so the birds could come out of their cage, perch up there, and fly across the room. I played Swamiji's music softly for them on the cd player. It made them sing so expressively. I spoke cheerfully to them and gave them loving attention. But, Soto still didn't want to be with us. He kept trying to make it out by the kitchen door.

Finally when Bob was building a bathroom onto the den, his covering plastic left a crack and Soto escaped. Mrs. Wiggins was inconsolable and chirped incessantly. We got another male; Django to soothe her. I didn't however, realize that I should have cleaned the little culverts more often. Mrs. Wiggins fell dead one day. Then we had the one bird again. We got another mate, then Django died after a time, and then we had the lone female. Months had turned into years, and I felt the anguishing monotony of being a bird and having to live in a den.

I know it probably wasn't that bad for them. But, in spite of all the comforts I provided them, and a nice clean cage, I couldn't help it. I was miserable that they couldn't be free. And, each time a bird had died or left, I wanted to call it quits, only to have to buy another one to be company for the lone survivor. I was stuck in a never ending cycle...

One day Bob came home with a little Russian Gray kitten from Robert's neighborhood. He had been found wondering the road and nobody there could take him. I knew this was an awful prospect; a kitten left outside with that dangerous road or inside with the birds. Grey cat stole my heart. He was a little person. He would lay on my chest when I meditated laying down. He would stretch his arms up around my neck when I picked him up. He would stand up and fall happily over like a puppet to make me laugh. His fur was the softest most beautiful blue grey color; rich and full. But, he had a gleam in his eye for those birds from the first moment he saw them. Then he was a leopard. We had to babysit the birds constantly. It was a horrible situation to be in. When we left the house, we would put Greycat in the laundry room and close the folding door. Well, one day we came home and both the birds had been slaughtered. Greycat had pawed the door open. He must have really terrorized them to have made them swoop low enough to catch them. How I grieved that I hadn't been able to protect my own birds.

Then, the den was peaceful. After a time I came to think that Greycat came as a direct universal law of karma for the birds to be set free at my urgence.* I finally began to feel a little better. Then Grey cat began leaving the yard, and crossing that dangerous road. I got that terrible feeling in my gut, and started to inwardly distance myself from him emotionally. When I saw him heading for the road, I would call. He would turn and look, then run to me for some love. But slowly he was breaking away. When I would call he would look longer; more thoughtfully, before returning to me. I knew he was weaning me. Then one day he never came back.

Finally this morning, it seems I can just follow my breath. Maitreyi from the Ananda website had stated a truth so eloquently and simply in a poem, that it has transferred into my psyche.

> "Of all trappings of desire of material will?
> Just follow your breath 'til your heart becomes still;
> You'll find such delights if you only knew,
> Right there, inside that person called, "You."

For the first time maybe, I cuddled back into the breath. It slowed my heart, then my heart slowed it, then it slowed my heart some more, and so on. I settled in with a sigh of relief, thinking to myself (paraphrasing Swamiji) Good bye scenes of this world. Colors, beauties, winding roads..I don't care about any of you. Goodbye meditation. You're not important..Goodbye.

Having developed my sensitivities somewhat through diligently magnetizing a flow of energy through the spine, I have effectively cleared out some 'effect' possibilities from various old causes. I then had a somewhat developed focus to make something happen to free the birds. More advanced devotees than I have power to attract circumstances very quickly, as there are no conflicting cross currents to disturb the will's magnetism toward an end. So, just as you may dream a whole scenario and control that, God's dream is controlled by him, and it us US. When we start guiding events consciously and not just subconsciously; having refined our natures enough to do so, then we are 'that'. We children are learning what Father can do. We only need to make a go of it and try; get on the path and take each first step until we get some progress under our belts. We will perfect the process more and more. Thus, finally "Thou art That". "Be ye therefore perfect as your father in Heaven is perfect". Jesus

Asha Praver: disciple since 1969 says of Swamiji when she met him—
He was invited to give a lecture at Stanford University. I went to hear him, and I have to say that it was his presence that spoke to me before he spoke. I was already a student of Self Realization of expanded Eastern kind of teachings, but I had never seen a living example of the principles I was studying. And, when he came into the room where he was to give his lecture, I sensed in his consciousness, the kind of freedom and bliss that I had been reading about but had never experienced. And, something in his consciousness touched mine immediately. —And then he spoke.

After he spoke I thought he was the most intelligent man I had ever heard speak.

But my commitment to him actually came from his consciousness before I even heard what he had to say.

If you always speak the truth, your words are such a determined and well directed force, that natural law yields to it; they are binding on the universe and manifest in intent.

A man with an incessant cough for 6 months or more, came to Swamiji.
The man didn't want to impose himself with this sickness, however, and remained upstairs. When Swamiji heard that he was not going to come down, he uttered "but he doesn't have a cough". It was suddenly and totally gone.

The thing about truth; it directs the lower elemental stages; the manifestations of thought, vibration, and matter adhere to it. For, in the highest state of consciousness; "Samadhi" (inner communion, enlightenment, or freedom), it is truth you experience.
Those that have learned how to access it and dwell within it, for example,
see 360 degrees around themselves, also up and down; everywhere. Someone could be making a gesture behind them, behind a wall, or even in a different country, and they could see it. They also perceive that they are "in" everything, or more accurately they "are" everything. They see that in truth they are not confined in one body, just as God isn't. God is truth and we are that. So, coming back out of Samadhi into a worldly duty, lets say, Paramahansa Nithyananda, (who goes into Samadhi often in the world today)
has stated that he did not feel to eat anything for days.
It was like he would have been taking a bite of himself!

When Swami Kriyananda talks of Yogananda (Master), he describes him as a perfect human being; not only this over-arching consciousness, but also this ability to relate completely appropriately with absolute sensitivity in all circumstances. Asha again:
My experience with Swami Kriyananda over these 40 years, has been this remarkable observation of right behavior. Right behavior not in the sense of social custom only or even particularly, but a sensitivity to the needs of others that never fails to perceive what people need and how to deliver it.

OVER THE EDGE

Not too long ago, I was dreaming that I was driving, and the steering went haywire. I had been having a re-occurring dream of this sort for some time too, where the hi-way would become dark, and I would be driving at a fast speed into complete and utter danger. While awake, I would prompt myself "just let Master take the wheel when that dream comes, and joyously let go. Maybe you will find the revelation that it is only a dream, and that will bring great freedom into it after you plunge over the edge".

In this dream, however, it didn't go dark. The steering or maybe the breaks quit working. Suddenly I was entering my house. There was turmoil there also. The house was a mess. It was bearing down on me that not only did I need to get the car fixed, but I needed to clean house. Then I realized my sister Robin, cousins Mooksie, Wendy, Sandy and some others had come to visit. That was a nice surprise, but I hurried around to get something for them to eat. I came up with some kind of weird olive and almond salad, and set it in front of Wendy. I was continuing to bustle about, when suddenly a warmth encompassed my heart. I stopped all my thinking and action, and just relaxed into the most blissful timelessness. Oh, I was going to enjoy this happy mess. I was so very content in this 'me' that I had found.

The teachings say that my liberation is a transformation to my own higher self. Master has given me Swamiji. But, ultimately I have to go on alone. I can't count on Swamiji and the others being at my meeting area forever. I will someday have to go beyond. We are all one, a vast expanse of consciousness. After I pass the idea of Swamiji, then I also have to leave Sharon. Do I have any way of doing this? Well, it's hard to say how it will work till I get there. But, I haven't been steered wrong this far.

I think of the man ascending the mountain who got stranded near the peak, unable to go up or down. He made it. His magnetism pulled him up a wall that turned out at an angle, not in. He didn't give up. He couldn't have pulled **himself** up any more than one can make themselves rise by pulling on his own bootstraps. He went straight to God for the lift.

Well, what then when we reach the part where nobody is in the abyss to help you, and it's just you reaching for God?

> Remember how when you were little and fell into the feeling of total contentment? Say your mom was busy, or your friends were ignoring you. The times you were able to go off and play without a further thought of it..well that's gotta be what it is. Absorb into this reality until it is not even you playing. Just a wonderful game of life being played by, for and with..whoever.

Place that thought into the spine for meditation. Say you don't feel Swamiji close by. You are trying, but your devotion is weak or unfocused. It's just too hazy. Well, go off and play. It's okay. Yes, you still want him of course. Just stay as close as you can in spirit. There are many reasons you can slip away from your guru. As long as you are in a human body, you are vulnerable of thinking of him the wrong way, for one thing. You may try to attach yourself somehow. That sets you apart for a time, again and again. Or your confidence may be lacking for some reason. A myriad of things can keep you from finding him on any given day. This leaves you discouraged.

But your only duty in life, the summit indeed of **all** these lives, is to find bliss, not the person of the guru. He is only there to help. You have to revert to that bare soul who is just naturally vibrant and content, without anybody or anything. Your desire has to become desireless for God alone. So, to achieve liberation or even to master death's final lesson, use **that** desire to break out like you always knew you could. Swamiji will be cheering you on. Blaze upward until you are disintegrated by the suns rays and melt into God.

AND I NEED YOU MORE THAN WANT YOU

AND I WANT YOU FOR ALL TIME

AND THE WITCHETA LINEMAN

IS STILL ON THE LINE   (jimmy webb)

Well, I'm not the county lineman. I am a bookblock editor mom and wife these days. But, when I listen to the words of this song and hear this line, I weep tears of the deepest longing. How long must this go on? Long enough to get me out of maya I hope. And what if I don't make it out? I'll have to return unaware as a baby again. I will have to wait for the time to be karmically right for my teachings to willow wisp in front of me once more, trying to catch my attention. What if I miss them? It's all too painful to consider. I may wonder off in the wrong direction, worst of all. How then to make the best use of my path, now that I have a foothold?

 I am a householder. Much of my work is outward, serving 2 teenagers and my husband. They just wouldn't understand the intricacies of what I'm studying. They are wonderful though, and serving them is such an honor. I try to keep healthy, for it is in my old age that I may be able to make sweeping inroads of progress, if I'm alone then and have the time. Then again, what if I drift off aimlessly having *too much* time? I just can't afford to think that way. I've made it this far and haven't missed meditation in almost 4 years since I've started. I've been more inspired at times than others of course, but always the pendulum swung back. My devotion always comes back to being very intense in time. And then 'my heart finds its morning and is refreshed'. Let me not be distracted by an easy row to hoe.

In fact meditating assures the row won't be easy. For a very good reason. When you meditate you become more and more attuned to God reminding activities. You dwell much more in love.

So when your daily activities take you into a worldly environment where there is tension, you sense your separateness from God much more keenly. God calls you back in this way.

In the natural law, you touch a hot stove and you get burned. In a similar way when a sincere devotee resorts to restlessness, it is God himself who exhorts "Whoa..come back here".

So it is a constant effort to stay focused. It may seem this play is unending. All the while you are so intently desiring to leave it all behind and find God. But, something will give, in time. Remember the parakeets and the Gray cat. Strong desire has its strong attraction. Something does indeed happen.

In the meantime, my uncle Peewee always said an apple tasted sweeter when you could snitch one off somebody's tree. The moments I am able to steal away at home for meditation too, are delicious.

It seems like life becomes harder and meditation easier when you learn in your meditative focus, how to emote joy inwardly; a kind of imploding rather than exploding. Then the outside world must by necessity start to become a meditation of sorts for you too. For, if you don't hone that focus in moments of everyday living, it will be a painful restlessness in comparison.

God draws you in ever closer. Perfect union with him someday will require no actions at all in an outer world. You won't ever have to come back then.

I find less and less the need to anticipate enlightenment. I am no longer worried about missing my chance were it to come. I have my practice. As long as I am doing that to the best of my ability, Master says it's like mathematics. Kriya yoga plus devotion equals God union. So, I don't think of missing my chance. It's like a gymnast being lifted to grab the brass ring. If you lift him a little and he's still far away, he'll have to lunge a distance to grab it. This would take some anticipation. But, I feel no such hurry. So, I will wait until I'm lifted right to the brass ring. Then I will just take it.

AT LAST IT WILL BE DONE

On the weekends I change up my meditation practice a bit. Instead of waking up the habitual time early in the morning, I just let aum wake me up in the middle of the night when it feels like it. Then I do a string of kriyas in that precious dark silence. Lately I've been thinking of it kind of like a tunnel of hope. It's like everybody from my environment; past or present, is in a prison. My present family too; my husband beside me on the bed, and the kids in their rooms . I wake to work on our tunnel out. It is a glorious job, because it is right action and is sanctioned very dearly by the Masters. So stone silent is the night, and hearing so keenly tuned to the task at hand through the expressive darkness. I am doing this secretly, so the breath has to be more quiet. Still, I adjust it to feel a cool steady surge up and a warm trickle down. When my husband stirs, I ease up so as not to wake him. Oh, he will be so happy when I surprise us one day with our freedom. Everything that happens during the week then, that is unsettling, is justified by my building of the freedom tunnel that I will open to all some sweet day.

Banat banat ban jai; doing,doing--At last it will be done.(LahiriMahasaya)

I had a close friend in my teens and early twenties. He had been in a renowned family pop group called "The Cowsills" in the sixties. He was the incredibly talented oldest sibling and founder; Billy. When I met him in Jasper Alberta,he said he had wondered off in a drunken stupor and ended up in Canada. I saw in the years to come, a twisted mix of genius and demons. Perhaps the sweetest man on earth was in a desperate battle with an evil power that wouldn't let go. We spent many peaceful weeks together on the road in Northern Alberta, singing in a duo together. We contentedly wondered down the road that led to each next town, just kind of melting into nature, and Billy took refuge.

 I was like a little sister to him. We studied music and artists we admired. He had known many of them, in fact. He showed me intricacies about singing harmonies and playing an infectious thumping rhythm on the guitar. I don't think anyone could have easily taken instruction from him though. He was a brute when in a mood. His upbraidings were so sharp as to slice you at the drop of a hat. You had to please him with your musical heart.

Just recently I saw this superlative performer as a teenage boy. At work here, I listen to Glen Campbell's version of Witcheta Lineman quite often on Utube. One day Billy's young face popped up in an ad on that site. The song was "The Rain, the Park and other Places". It was my favorite Cowsill song, (their other hits were "Indian Lake" and "Hair") but I had never seen a video on it. Clicking on it, I was moved to tears to see my beloved friend as a boy, singing with all those little facial expressions I knew so well. My tears were the most joyous laughter (for he was such a ham), and the most melencholic longing, at the same time.

Well, a few years after we had been singing together back in the 70's, he had moved to Vancouver, to the coast. One time I longed so to see him, that I set out for Vancouver from the Valley; a trip of some three hundred miles. Upon arriving, I had no idea where to go. It wasn't the weekend yet, but I asked around for a little joint that might have a good songwriter or small groovy group playing, and proceeded to find the place. I got there to find Billy. In the whole city, that was the place. We got up on the stage and sweetly sang an Everly Brothers song together. The crowd was captured. We then spent the remainder of the night quietly talking.

 I was to sing with him every now and then after that, but for the most part, I was to be separated from him for many years. His health got bad in his late fifties. Poor Billy, I expect those last years were especially torturous for him. He had abused himself so badly.

When I heard of his death, I was tossed into a whirlwind of grief. In the middle of the night, Bob and I heard a great crash.

In the morning we saw the mess that had been made in a closet where a wire shelf had given way, and my cassette tapes were scattered all over the floor; maybe 100 of them. I came home from work later that day, and Bob handed me a cassette. "Here", he said. "I picked it up because I thought it had my name on it;

'Bobby Crowell'. But it says 'Billy Cowsill'".

I put it in the tape player.

"Hi Shaye" It was Billy's bright voice. He proceeded to sing me four songs intersperced with a little conversation, just playing his guitar casually. It was recorded before a show he had been performing in Nashville when he had visited about 10 years earlier. He was, I knew, calming his nerves by making me this tape. Singing to me. His sense of humor was wonderful, but there was bitter sweet longing in the lyrics. At the end he leaned into the tape recorder and whispered "Bye Shaye..see you at the show".

LIKE A BIRD ON A WIRE

LIKE A DRUNK IN A MIDNIGHT CHOIR

I HAVE TRIED   IN MY WAY   TO BE FREE   (lenoard cohen)

(See you at the show Billy)

So precious is this flow of grace within my meditation this morning; that feeling of well being from which right action can spring forth from. Sometimes after a couple of hours at work though, I wonder where it went. I must better guard my dearly begotten. It trickles out through the cracks into this worldly place. I need to hold it tight to the spine. Carefully, even greedily so. For what when someone could use to be near a saint. I have been in contact with a powerful saint. I must serve that need. Even though I may not feel worthy of such a task, in this battle ground, there are few even seeking God. I may be your only hope at this most important of moments. Here is the liquid gold, just like sunshine. I have saved some just for you. Here, take of my bread and eat.

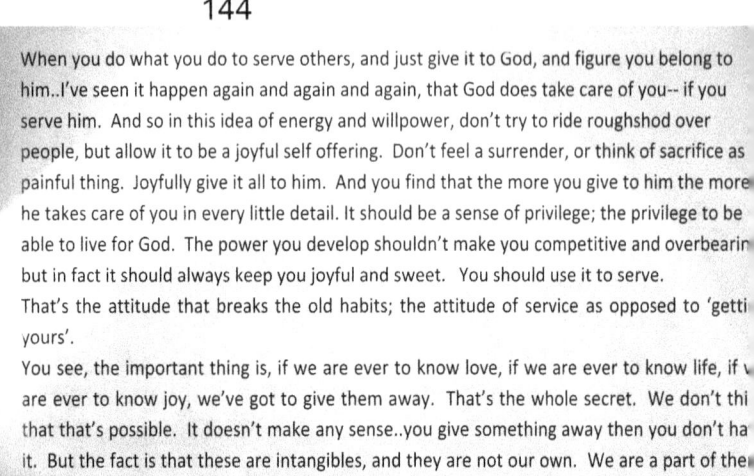

When you do what you do to serve others, and just give it to God, and figure you belong to him..I've seen it happen again and again and again, that God does take care of you-- if you serve him. And so in this idea of energy and willpower, don't try to ride roughshod over people, but allow it to be a joyful self offering. Don't feel a surrender, or think of sacrifice as painful thing. Joyfully give it all to him. And you find that the more you give to him the more he takes care of you in every little detail. It should be a sense of privilege; the privilege to be able to live for God. The power you develop shouldn't make you competitive and overbearin but in fact it should always keep you joyful and sweet. You should use it to serve.
That's the attitude that breaks the old habits; the attitude of service as opposed to 'getti yours'.
You see, the important thing is, if we are ever to know love, if we are ever to know life, if are ever to know joy, we've got to give them away. That's the whole secret. We don't thi that that's possible. It doesn't make any sense..you give something away then you don't ha it. But the fact is that these are intangibles, and they are not our own. We are a part of the They exist independently of us and they exist everywhere. And it's only as we are able attune ourselves with that infinite and recognize that *that* is the reality; see, when you give away, where are you giving it to? Into the infinite. You're affirming the infinite is your reality not the little ego. You've got to make that affirmation if you're ever to achieve infinite cosmic consciousness. So learn to give service, learn to give joy, learn to give the energy th you have to the welfare of others.
And then, you'll become more and more conscious of it as not being your energy only, but th energy you can draw on from the infinite; that energy flowing through you. And then, relax and feel. Withdraw that energy within yourself and become aware of that source, and offer that source upward into the infinite.
Joy to you all.
Swamiji was talking about how great composers felt the flow coming through them; they wer only a channel, versus not so great composers who believed they conceived their works. The he took it down to the level of everyday actions:There's still the flow of the divine in doing something perfectly mundane. And that's what we all need to get. And we have to rigidly school ourselves not to allow that thought to come in that I did it. For two reasons; one is bondage. It's just not in your own interest. It feels good on a certain level to think "I'm prett good", but then suddenly you realize it doesn't feel good at all; it feels unclean. You feel trapped. You feel bound by this little body when there's something in the nature of the soul that wants to be in all bodies. It doesn't want to be stuck in some little form. And as soon as you emphasize "I did it", you're emphasizing your limitation. We need to have the experienc of going through the test of doing what we can to the best of our ability and letting God be th doer. That is how we grow.
By not experiencing this practice, we remain children. We have to achieve freedom by victor and not by avoidance; not by fear.But the reason it's very much in our interest to accept that we're not *in it*, is that we become free this way. And no other way.You have to work on yourself; you have to discipline yourself because the ego doesn't like to give the credit to somebody else, and it's thinking that God is somebody else. What we need to do is break tha hypnosis and understand that he's ourself and that we don't exist except for him.True humill is getting our self out of the way and say God is the doer.You can't do anything but God can c everything.However, he can't do anything at all except through instruments.And "to those who love greatly much is forgiven"(Jesus). Love is the most important thing that will win God's grace to you. Not because he's flattered because you love him. But because you by your love put yourself in a receptive frame so that he can give you that which he longs to give

(Swamiji in a 5 day talk on the chakras)   audio reading of this page featured on included cd

GUIDING ARJUNA'S CHARIOT

Years ago I had a dream that I met the devil. I hadn't really had to put my hand to the plow yet in life, and I thought I could take him on. He manifested as a roaring mad horse speeding toward me like a freight train in a dark open field, with thunder and lightning animating the sky. At the last moment of his approach I tricked him and swerved aside. He missed me. But, then, to my dismay, I found every time I turned around there he was. I soon found I didn't have the stamina to continue, and he was only getting stronger..

Well, Master, I have trained for many things in this life. None of them brought me fulfillment, really. But in my sports, music, my programming on the computer, I peeled back each layer and eagerly bore deeper trying to get to the source, to know all I could possibly know. I knew you couldn't know it all, but I was driven. I knew there must be a reason to try. When each undertaking in turn, showed itself to no longer be my direction in life, I thought "alright. At least I have done it." I had begun to think I was getting old; winding down, when my path turned abruptly to an about face, facing you.

I was a little dull at first. It was like coming out of a long sleep. I thought 'I must do this, though I have no idea how'. But I was desperate to find you at that point. I began to see you had softly closed the doors of my other studies, when their time of usefulness had been fulfilled. I got too old to have the competitive edge in sports. Writing songs had become mechanical. I lost my record deal at Capitol records, and had been so disillusioned with the music business. You let it break my heart dear Lord, so that my heart might grow back stronger.

I became entranced with programming; visual basic, databases, and html web programming. I think I was trying to get away from people, and the language was so intriguing. There was a certain power to be felt in manipulating an inanimate object to get a vast array of coherent information at your fingertips. But, it wasn't my true path either, and you didn't open up any doors for a job in that arena. Thus I got my bookblock editing job, that takes some expertise, but is mostly just humble, good work. And some of it is repetitious enough that I can do it while studying Swamiji's books, lessons, speeches and music with my headphones on. I have heard his voice so much in the last 3 or 4 years, that it has become my beacon of hope. I meditate 3 times every day.

I am now in the habit, even though it became a bit of a chore at first. But when I started having those little inklings one gets when a lively penetrating power starts flowing up the spine, things start to come more easily.

You have whispered to me "this is what you must put all your dedication into now." It has become a feverish love for me because you are in it. Swamiji spoke of seeing the dew drop on a flower pedal, and knowing that the beauty is overwhelming. Why can't I feel it! I must! I go into the spine and I find any way I can to consciously permeate through there with the relaxation, the focus, the brilliance, and yes..the happiness above all. I bring inspirations up as close as I can in the spiritual eye and I thrive on them. I bow before them. I am thankful for them. I offer them to God. Each day I dedicate the time to go within this spine that is becoming my home, and give my spirit its exercise up and down, generating magnetism. I feed it throughout the day, stay close to it and nurture it.

Sometimes I take extra time to stop at each chakra and concentrate on the inroads we're building through them. I try to dissolve blockages, and get the trickle moving. I put a searchlight of love up in there as close and wide as I can get it, and hold it there with great hope, letting the Masters meet it with the grace it calls for. It thrills to the attention. Stronger and stronger it is getting; this flow within me. And someday, it will get me out of here. Someday it will break loose of this old body, soaring all the way out, projected like a happy burst of sunlight, and I will be home. Home, like I had never been gone.

This time, in my final great undertaking of this lifetime, I will not reach outward. I will not become prideful, or even curious about the outside. This is it. This is the test for which all the other trainings were merely practice. This is my time. Do I have it all under my belt? I hope so. My preparation has served me well I think, in that with all my subjects of deep study, what I was always in a deeper sense trying to master was the art of being the best I could be on demand; at any given moment. To be able to call upon that grit you've developed; that unbridled power of love itself, which gives each situation what it needs.

 A bull rider described it well on TV the other night. The announcer asked him why he'd been falling short of his usually high scoring rides. "You know," he said thoughtfully, "I used to think 'How can I squeeze the best ride out of each one of my 8 seconds on this bull'. Now I have caught myself thinking 'What can I do to stay on this bull for 8 seconds''. There's a big difference.

A boxer we saw too, got knocked out in the ring. They were slapping his face, and giving him smelling salts. When he started to stir, his coach asked him "Do you know where you are?"

"I'm in one hell of a fight!" he said.

What I have gathered up in me for this fight is gona have to do. With God's grace, it will be enough. Thankfully, I have a secret weapon; Swamiji's music. It calms me, and that is my lifeline. I have stepped onto this path again, this time through hell or high water I will realize it is here and turn to it as my only love. My whole focus is here now. I have a few good years left. I have to live them **any**way, and now I have a burning desire to live them in the **right** way.

Krishna, before exhorting Arjuna to do battle spoke "as if smiling"

Swami Kriyananda is reading from his audio book of the 'Essence of the Bhagavad Gita', explained by Paramahansa Yogananda:

"This phrase, Yogananda said, is important. Because it indicates that God is no stern judge of human behavior, but is on **our side**. He wants us to advance spiritually and forever forgives us if we err. The words "**as if smiling**" indicate that Arjuna has already advanced far on the path, to win such an indication of God's love. As Krishna remains inactive during the war, and participates only to guide Arjuna's chariot, so he often seems remote to the devotee, and even *indifferent* to the most earnest efforts to attain him.

Krishna's smile, however (Swamijis voice softens, and breaks with emotion) is ever there .. for those who seek him, ..earnestly. It is not easily won but loving reassurance is given from time to time in one form or another. The Devotee feels Gods loving support in his heart. In time he is conscious of that inward smile. It is with this smile, that Krishna gives his discourse, in the Bhavagad Gita. It is with sweetest love, that God exhorts the devotee to seek him unconditionally as the only source of fulfillment there is"

Glowing in your face   flowing in your eyes
how my thoughts embrace   what beyond here lies

oh my heart deliver me   what else can I do
for my journey has to find it's end in you

tranquil ocean deep   see with every mile
how far I've come   to see you smile

Moving from the bay   back into the tide
I will make my way   to the world inside

For this hunger born of you   to ever find it's rest
I must give my all and do my very best

when it shines on me   all will be worth while
how far I've come   to see you smile

through the darkened caverns lost
wilted and withdrawn
I will yet rise to reach beyond

ocean I will be   no more little isle
how far I've come   to see you smile

(sharon's Christmas song to Swami Kriyananda)

the end

Finally, one last entry. I went on a backpacking trip in April with some Ananda people, to the scenic Point Reyes Park in California, north of San Francisco. It was so very beautiful. I was delirious with love for God. Upon leaving the last morning, we were expressing what we saw in the hills there by the ocean. I suddenly saw Yogananda's face beaming out from behind them, fading into the sky. But it was kind of like Mount Rushmore; four of these faces, all his, bigger than life, were blanketing my view there.

Then, this weekend when I had to make a cover for this book, I hurriedly came up with a concept, and when I was finished, there was the vision. His face there behind the foxhole mountain, was what I had seen. What a blessing to have you surrounding me the way you do, Dearest Sir. As I say in the beginning of this book, I don't know what I have done to attract your protection this way. Oh, I love you so very much.

Swamiji has written 140-some books and over 400 pieces of music.
At the time of this writing Swami Kriyananda is 84 years old, still teaching extensively out of his 8 Ananda communities around the world, from India, to Italy, and throughout the USA. Ananda village is 1000 acres nestled in the foothills of the Sierra Nevada mountains in California. It is my sanctuary. www.ananda.org.

The "As If Smiling" audio CD sleeve Companion Songs & Commentaries
can be downloaded for free from the audio books tab at www.SharonLenoreAnderson.com

The Only Tree	from	pg. 6
Blue	from	pg. 14
My Jesus	from	pg. 17
Gethsemane	from	pg. 19
Candle	from	pg. 20
Forever	from	pg. 23
Valley of Forgiveness	from	pg. 26
Uncle	from	pg. 32
Heavenly Love	from	pg. 39
I Got That from You	from	pg. 41
Indian Eyes	from	pg. 51
Springtime Johnny	from	pg. 67
Born to Be	from	pg. 70
Out of My Heart	from	pg. 105
Morning Song	from	pg. 107
Your Little Girl	from	pg. 110
Kriyananda	from	pg. 127
Angel	from	pg. 131
To See You Smile	from	pg. 148
Commentaries	pgs. 18, 132, 144, 147	

www.ingramcontent.com/pod-product-compliance
Lightning Source LLC
Chambersburg PA
CBHW050539300426
44113CB00012B/2179